Christian Leadership

Christian Leadership

John Perry

HODDER AND STOUGHTON
LONDON SYDNEY AUCKLAND TORONTO

British Library Cataloguing in Publication Data

Perry, John
  Christian leadership.
  1. Christian life
  I. Title
  248.4   BV4501.2

ISBN 0 340 27803 X

Printed in Great Britain for Hodder and Stoughton Limited, Mill Road, Dunton Green, Sevenoaks, Kent by Richard Clay (The Chaucer Press) Ltd, Bungay, Suffolk. Filmset in Monophoto Times by Northumberland Press Ltd, Gateshead. Hodder and Stoughton Editorial Office: 47 Bedford Square, London WC1B 3DP.

CONTENTS

PREFACE

At a centre like Lee Abbey, which each year welcomes several thousand guests — clergy and laity — questions of church growth or decline are constantly under discussion. Time and time again the key issue is found to be leadership.

In the final analysis it is the quality of leadership in the local church that makes all the difference. If churches, however small, are given strong, sensitive and visionary leadership a clear sense of purpose is apparent. On the other hand, where positive leadership is not in evidence a lack of cohesion and direction is inevitable. Even the best schemes for church growth come to nothing unless there is the right kind of leadership to ensure their implementation.

My aim in this book is to encourage the discovery and development of leadership at every level in the life of the local church. At the same time, I have tried to explore and face the difficulties, temptations and tensions, as well as the wide-ranging opportunities, that Christian leadership presents. For convenience 'he' rather than 'he or she' has generally been used. The principles are equally applicable to everyone.

There are few better schools for Christian leadership than a large family. I owe more than I can say to the love and friendship of my wife, Gay, and our family of five — Karen, Andrew, Timothy, Susanni and Jonathan. In turn, we belong to the even larger family of the Lee Abbey Community. I count it as an enormous privilege to be their leader. Expressions of gratitude are incomplete without paying tribute to my secretary, Lyn Walker, who has typed the manuscript, and Leanne Van Dyk, who has carefully checked its contents.

John Perry

Chapter 1

THE PARAMOUNT REQUIREMENT

I begin with a confession. For a number of years I have been addicted to anything that comes from the pen of the novelist Morris West. Always meticulous in his research, he writes perceptively and, at times, prophetically, on issues and events in a way that grips, disturbs and excites his readers. In one of his earlier books, *The Shoes of the Fisherman*, the Cardinals ask the newly-elected Pope ... 'Quid vobis videtur ... What do you want?' He replies, 'Find me men with fire in their hearts and wings on their feet'.[1]

What astute insight! In his search for leaders in his Church, God is always on the look out for people who have the fire of the Spirit in their hearts and the wings of obedience on their feet. He delights to use those who acknowledge their constant and complete dependence on him and are willing to accept the challenge of leadership.

When we trace through the pages of the Bible we find many illustrations of men and women, called to positions of leadership, being prepared and strengthened by the Spirit of God. Their inadequacy matched by his adequacy; their powerlessness by his powerfulness. In their weakness we see them made strong by the limitless resources of God.

Joshua and Gideon

To Joshua fell the awesome task of assuming the mantle of his mentor, Moses, and leading the Israelites into the Promised Land. Joshua was a man who possessed many of the natural qualities of leadership. Moreover, Moses had carefully groomed him as his successor. Yet in his own strength Joshua knew that the job was far too big for him. He had learnt from watching Moses that the only answer was a close relationship with a God who offered his friendship, wisdom and strength to those prepared to trust and obey him. Consequently, the Israelites recognised and accepted Joshua's leadership because they saw the fire of the Spirit in his heart and the wings of obedience on his feet, 'Joshua son of Nun was filled with the spirit of wisdom because Moses had laid his hands on him. So the Israelites listened to him and did what the Lord had commanded Moses.' (Deut. 34:9).

Unlike Joshua, Gideon had few apparent qualities for leadership. No selection board would have looked at him twice. We first meet him in Judges Chapter 6, furtively threshing wheat in the winepress to hide it from the marauding Midianites. When the angel of the Lord appeared to Gideon and greeted him with the words, 'The Lord is with you mighty warrior', Gideon was completely nonplussed. Not only did he believe that the Lord had deserted Israel but any suggestion that he might be her deliverer seemed ridiculous. After all, he belonged to the weakest clan and was regarded as of little account in his own family. But this was the man that God chose to restore the nation's morale and bring her victory over her enemies.

With much fear and trepidation Gideon put himself in the hands of God. In turn, 'The Spirit of the Lord came upon Gideon' (v. 34). A more literal translation would be, 'The Spirit of the Lord clothed himself with Gideon.' He became the garment of the Holy Spirit.

> The Holy Spirit clothed himself
> It makes the record say
> 'with Gideon';
> So, he became
> As nothing in the fray.
> But a suit of working clothes
> the Spirit wore that day!

The hardest lesson to accept and learn about Christian leadership is that it has to be in God's strength and not our own. Other qualifications for leadership are necessary but the primary qualification is a recognition that God's work must be done in his way and with his power. This cuts right across the accepted attitude, 'I can do this in my own strength.' It questions the more normal approach to ambition and achievement. Yet this is the way God chooses to work. That is why those who feel they have little to offer to God are often surprised beyond measure by what he is able to do in and through them. God chooses the weak things of the world to shame the strong.

In *Letters from the Desert*, Carlo Carretto shares his struggle over the years to admit his weakness and powerlessness. He describes his attempt to appear in public with 'a nice mask of self-assurance'. Gradually however, God made him face up to his inadequacy and his need of a power greater than his own. 'Now I contrast my powerlessness with the powerfulness of God, the heap of my sins with the completeness of his mercy. And I place the abyss of my smallness beneath the abyss of his greatness. God can do everything, and I can do nothing, but if I offer this nothing in prayer to God, everything becomes possible in me.'[2]

Jesus's Manifesto

When presenting his account of the events that heralded the ministry of Jesus, Luke took great care to emphasise the action of the Holy Spirit. The Spirit that came upon Jesus at his baptism then led him into the desert where for forty days he was tempted by the devil. Afterwards 'Jesus returned to Galilee in the power of the Spirit' ('armed with the Spirit' (4:14, NEB). On the Sabbath he went to the synagogue in his own town of Nazareth and was given the scroll of the prophet Isaiah to read. Deliberately he chose to read the passage from Chapter 61:

> The Spirit of the Lord is on me,
> because he has anointed me

11

> to preach good news to the poor.
> He has sent me to proclaim
> freedom for the prisoners
> and recovery of sight for the blind,
> to release the oppressed,
> to proclaim the year of the Lord's favour.
>
> (vv. 18–19)

When he sat down the eyes of everyone were fixed on the carpenter's son who had read with such authority. 'Today', Jesus said, 'this scripture is fulfilled in your hearing' (v. 21). In unmistakable terms Jesus had declared the manifesto which was to launch him into his ministry and mission. With the fire of the Spirit in his heart and the wings of obedience to the will of the Father on his feet, he began his work. There was to be no turning back.

The Early Church

To those whom he chose as his disciples and who would become the first leaders of the early Church, Jesus promised all the help they needed. He fully understood their frailty and fears and had no intention of leaving them to cope on their own. No task would be too great, no opposition too strong. He would provide for his disciples the same power that had been given to him. 'I am going to send you what my Father has promised; but stay in the city until you have been clothed with power from on high' (Luke 24:49). With the dawning of the day of Pentecost the promise of Jesus was unforgettably fulfilled. The disciples were all filled and equipped with the Holy Spirit.

The stirring account of the early Church in the Acts of the Apostles repeatedly illustrates that leadership was given to those whose lives bore the marks of the Spirit. For example, when the Apostles were looking for seven men for the practical oversight and care of widowed Grecian Jews, they gave instructions that those chosen should be known to be 'full of the Spirit and wisdom' (Acts 6:3). Whether it was an apostle 'preaching the word of God' or someone appointed for the 'daily distribution of food', the expectation was the same – to have the fire of the Spirit in their hearts.

What a difference it would make to the life of every church if these same criteria for responsibility and leadership were applied, that those who teach children, lead a youth club, a women's meeting or a home group, administer the funds or serve on the church council, should be chosen because they are known to be 'full of the Spirit and wisdom'. If leadership at every level of the local Church was stamped by the sign and seal of the Spirit, the change would be noticeable and often remarkable.

One thing is certain. When we know our need of God's grace and strength for Christian service and leadership, we soon realise that we have to go on being filled and fired by the Spirit. D. L. Moody was once asked if he was filled with the Spirit. 'Yes', he replied, 'but I leak!' Conscious that they might begin to 'leak' as a result of increased pressure from the Jewish authorities, Peter and John and the other apostles prayed for great boldness to speak God's word. What they asked for, they received. 'After they prayed, the place where they were meeting was shaken. And they were all filled with the Holy Spirit and spoke the word of God boldly' (Acts 4:31).

'Tsholla Mawo Gago Jesu'

On a sunny, sultry day in November 1980, my wife and I were taking part in a multiracial conference for clergy and lay leaders in South Africa. Many of them had travelled considerable distances in order to attend the conference held at Pietersburg in the Northern Transvaal. They eagerly welcomed the opportunity for fellowship and teaching. During a time of worship one of the black clergy began to sing, *'Tsholla Mawo Gago Jesu* – Pour down your Spirit, Jesus.' Soon everyone joined him. It was an unforgettable moment and a timely reminder to us all that effective Christian leadership must be in the power of the Holy Spirit.

Chapter 2

THE PATTERN TO FOLLOW

For the suburban and city dweller, the serene pastoral picture of a shepherd with his flock can seem somewhat incongruous. Yet, on more careful reflection, the shepherd and his sheep provide many practical pointers for leadership within the local church, whatever its geographical location. Furthermore, Jesus used the analogy of a shepherd and his sheep to describe his relationship to his followers. He who said, 'I am the good shepherd' (John 10:11) provides the perfect pattern for Christian leadership.

Under Authority

The Christian leader is an under-shepherd, submitting to the authority of Jesus Christ the Chief Shepherd. Jesus himself lived a life of absolute obedience to the will of his Father. This was his supreme aim. 'I have come down from heaven not to do my will but to do the will of him who sent me' (John 6:38). It was in his complete submission that Jesus found his own spiritual authority and power. This was why he was enormously impressed by the faith of the centurion who came to him about his sick servant. As the soldier explained, 'I myself am a man under authority, with soldiers under me. I tell this one, "Go", and he goes; and that one, "Come", and he comes. I say to my servant, "Do this", and he does it' (Luke 7:8).

I believe it is profoundly true that only those who have learnt to obey and come under the authority of God, and of others, can exercise leadership with any authority. Leadership is abused when it is in the hands of the headstrong and the 'know it all'. Unless we have first accepted the yoke of Christ and learnt to be led, we can never be fit to lead others.

The greater the responsibilities entrusted to us, the greater our reliance on the Shepherd Lord whom we serve.

When he was enthroned as Bishop of Manchester, William Temple — later to become Archbishop of Canterbury — spoke these simple and memorable words:

I come as a learner, with no policy to advocate, no plan already formed to follow. But I come with one burning desire; it is that in all our activities, sacred and secular, ecclesiastical and social, we should help each other to fix our eyes on Jesus, making him our only guide ... Pray for me, I ask you, not chiefly that I may be wise and strong, or any such thing, though for these things I need your prayers. But pray for me chiefly that I may never let go of the unseen hand of the Lord Jesus and may live in daily fellowship with him. It is so that you will most of all help me to help you.

What can the Christian leader, as an under-shepherd, learn from Jesus?

Knowing

Jesus said, 'I am the good shepherd; I know my sheep and my sheep know me — just as the Father knows me and I know the Father ...' (John 10:14). If we saw a flock of sheep in the Middle East all the sheep would look the same. However, if their shepherd was a good one, he would know each one individually and would have his own special name for every one of them. The sheep would know their shepherd and would know that he cared for them twenty-four hours a day. They would trust him implicitly. They would respond to his voice and follow his lead.

This is the example Jesus chose to describe his relationship with his followers. In the same way, the leader must know those he leads, not only know about them, but know them personally — their strengths and weaknesses, their hopes and fears. One farmer's wife wrote to express deep disappointment that her vicar didn't seem to know her when she came to church and said, 'On this subject of recognition my husband keeps 500 ewes and somehow knows each one, incredible though it may seem!'

An increasing number of people in society today feel that their lives are of little significance, whether in the place they work or in their local community. They have no sense of 'belonging'. It is to this deep human longing to be known, loved and wanted that the Church of Jesus Christ can gladly and confidently respond. In the eyes of God everyone matters and the local church has an unparalleled opportunity to show it.

When Pope John Paul II was a cardinal, he spoke at a conference in Rome on the ever-growing depersonalisation of man. 'I don't mean only the danger of considering man as a mere instrument of production. I mean the even greater danger that man himself, more or less consciously, is beginning to see himself as a passive element on a production line, subject to any or every kind of manipulation. If contemporary human progress is to have a truly human face, then it must seek to provide man not only with a means of obtaining the material necessities of life but also with the opportunity of becoming more human. Unless it can achieve that, progress can only increase the feeling of alienation.'

At the heart of true pastoral caring is the conviction that every human being is unique and invaluable. I think of those whom I have known and worked with who have given themselves tirelessly as Sunday School teachers or youth leaders. They would spend long hours visiting their youngsters in their homes or preparing events that would add extra bite to the adventure of following Christ. They went after those who had got out of touch and sought to encourage them back. They loved and prayed for each boy and girl in their care. Nothing was too much trouble; no sacrifice was too great. Like Jesus, they knew their sheep and their sheep knew them.

Feeding

The good shepherd will ensure that his sheep are well fed and watered. Jesus had compassion on the crowds because they were like sheep without shepherds who knew and fed them. Unlike the Pharisees, Jesus taught with authority and his words were received hungrily. They were words of life and of hope. Yet they were not always palatable. On one occasion, Jesus spelt out the costliness of discipleship and many turned away. Rather wearily, Jesus turned to the disciples. 'You do not want to leave too, do you?' Simon Peter answered for them all. 'Lord, to whom shall we go? You have the words of eternal life. We believe and know that you are the Holy One of God.' (John 6:67–9).

The under-shepherd has the privilege and responsibility of feeding the flock of Christ. Yet I see overwhelming evidence that many congregations are on minimum rations. We soon feel the effects if we never have a square meal and exist on snacks. But snacks are the diet of many in the local church today. Instead of growing up strong and mature in Christ, far too many Christians, young and old, are spiritually weak and emaciated. Untaught, they are unsure of their spiritual foundations. It is little wonder that they lack the confidence or even the desire to share their faith with others.

The onus to take preaching and teaching far more seriously is not only upon the clergy but upon all who have any part in teaching the Christian faith to others. In the past the majority of young people grew up with some kind of 'God-framework' because of Christian teaching received in school and at home. This is no longer the case. There is widespread ignorance of the basic facts of Christianity and its application to daily living. How important, therefore, that young people who are in touch with the local church receive the quality of teaching and help that they need. The situation is urgent.

Whether it be teaching a group of children or young people, leading a home group, or preaching from a pulpit, the question to answer is, 'Am I preparing and offering a meal or a

17

snack?' The meal must match the capacity and the circumstances but the food must be good and be imaginatively presented.

The Great Shepherd also feeds us through sacrament as well as by word. When we stretch out empty hands to receive the tokens of Christ's love in the sacrament of his body and blood, he feeds and nourishes us. Our guests at Lee Abbey often comment on the added significance this sacrament has had for them when they are addressed by their Christian name as they are given the bread and wine. In this simple way the personal love of Christ is affirmed as they feed by faith upon him.

Tending

The caring shepherd would be concerned about the bumps and bruises of his sheep. He would search for the sheep that had got caught up in a thicket, stranded on a rock, and would carry it home tenderly on his shoulders so that the process of healing could begin. Peter had seen the tender compassion of Jesus in his care for others — the lepers and the lame, the blind and the bereaved, the sinners and the sinned-against. What is more, he himself had experienced his master's tender love, mercy and forgiveness in the abyss of failure. When writing later to others who had the responsibilities of leadership, he encourages them, 'Tend the flock of God that is your charge, not by constraint but willingly, not for shameful gain but eagerly, not as domineering over those in your charge but being examples to the flock.' (1 Pet. 5:2–3, RSV).

Religious leaders who were more concerned for their own ease than for the welfare of their people often came under the forthright condemnation of the Old Testament prophets.

This is what the Sovereign Lord says: Woe to the shepherds of Israel who only take care of themselves! Should not shepherds take care of the flock? You eat the curds, clothe yourselves with the wool and slaughter the choice animals, but you do not take care of the flock. You have not strengthened the weak or healed the sick or bound up the injured. You have not brought back the strays or searched for the lost. You have ruled them harshly and brutally.'

(Ezek. 34:2–4)

Within each church and local community there are increasing numbers of people for whom caring leaders can bring hope and healing in the name of the Good Shepherd. The fractured family, the unemployed, the lonely and fearful, will be among them. By their own example, Christian leaders can in turn help those they lead to express the tending love of Jesus to others. As Lesslie Newbigin has written, 'The Church is not an organisation of spiritual giants. It is broken men and women who can lead others to the Cross.'[3]

Guarding

The good shepherd would guard his sheep with his life. At night he would lie across the gateway of the pen to protect the sheep from wild beasts or robbers. If need be, he would be ready to sacrifice his life. Jesus described himself as 'the gate for the sheep' (John 10:7) and as 'the good shepherd who lays down his life for his sheep' (v. 15).

Watchfulness must be one of the chief hallmarks of the under-shepherd's attitude to those he leads. 'Guard yourselves and all the flock of which the Holy Spirit has made you over-seers.' Paul warned the Ephesian elders (Acts 20:28). The order is important. One of the greatest dangers in Christian leadership is to be so pre-occupied with leading and caring for others that we neglect our own paramount need to keep our eyes fixed on Jesus Christ on whom our faith depends from start to finish. We are of little use to anyone if we become detached from the Chief Shepherd. The penetrating words of Richard Baxter are an uncomfortable reminder, not only to the preacher but to all who would shepherd the flock of Christ, that they must first guard themselves:

See that the work of saving grace is thoroughly wrought in your own souls. Take heed to yourselves lest you be void of that saving grace of God which you offer to others and be strangers to the effectual working of that Gospel which you preach; lest while you proclaim the necessity of a Saviour to the world, your own heart should neglect him and his saving benefits. Take heed to yourselves lest you perish while you call upon others to take heed of perishing; lest you famish yourselves while you prepare their food.[4]

Only the leader who guards his own relationship with Christ so that it grows and deepens will be alert enough to guard the flock which the Holy Spirit has placed in his care.

A vitally important part of the flock which needs to be tended and guarded is the leader's own family. We are to be shepherds to our partners and children. Many a Christian home has come to grief or been placed under intolerable strain because the care of the family has been neglected. I shall not forget a minister coming to see me in great distress because his wife had left him. He had realised too late that though he had been assiduous in his care of others in his congregation, he had not cared enough for his wife and children.

In the opening chapter of his autobiography, *Testament of Faith*, William Barclay pays a glowing tribute to his wife, Kate, for the constant support and encouragement she had given him in over forty years of marriage.[5] There is, though, a touch of sadness which many a Christian leader — not only clergy — will echo. 'As I come near to the end of my days, the one thing that haunts me more than anything else is that I've been so unsatisfactory a husband and a father. As the Song of Solomon has it: "They made me keeper of the vineyards; but my own vineyard I have not kept." ' When the Pastoral Epistles are laying down the qualifications for the elder, the deacon and the bishop, one of the unvarying demands is that 'he must know how to manage his own household' — and for a minister that is the hardest thing in the world.

'Guard your marriage' was a word of warning given to us on our wedding day. On a number of occasions during the years that have followed we have needed to heed these wise words. Husbands need to be pastors to their own wives and families. Couples need to care and make time for one another and for their children. In this way the strength and joys of family life that have their roots deep down in the love of God can fully blossom. With the alarming acceleration in the breakdown of family life, the consistently loving witness of the Christian home can provide an anchor of hope in a turbulent, drifting society.

When we came down to North Devon to join the Lee Abbey Community, a member of our congregation gave me a shepherd's crook as a parting gift. It was certainly appropriate. In this part of the country the woolly variety far outnumber the human breed! Propped up in a corner of my study the crook is a constant reminder to a very fallible under-shepherd that he is to know, feed, tend and guard the flock of God.

Chapter 3

TAKING THE TOWEL

A knock on our vicarage door announced the arrival of the Bishop of Hertford, John Trillo, and his wife, Pat — an hour before they were expected for a meal followed by a confirmation service. An afternoon engagement in the area had finished early so they had come straight on to us. 'What can we do to help?' was their first question. Within a few minutes Pat was on her knees in the bathroom bathing two of our children.

If leadership is about shepherding, it is also about serving. Some of the most profound examples of leadership are seen in humble, unobtrusive acts of caring that reflect a spirit of selfless love. Where leadership in the church dominates rather than serves, it is completely alien to the whole tenor of the New Testament.

Doulos

There are two principal Greek words used for servant in the New Testament: *doulos* and *diakonos*. The word *doulos* is a relationship word and means literally a 'slave', one who belongs lock, stock and barrel to someone else. The slave had no rights of his own. In this sense, Paul could write to the Philippians and say of himself and Timothy that they were 'servants of Christ' (1:1). Their relationship to Jesus as Lord was one of total commitment. In the same vein the Apostle wrote, 'You are not your own; you were bought at a price. Therefore honour God with your body' (1 Cor. 6:19–20). This language from the slave market is a vivid reminder of one important aspect of the

Christian's relationship to his Master. He is a bond slave of Christ to whom he gladly gives his love and allegiance. Why? Because in the service of Jesus true freedom is found.

I think of a man in his early fifties who had spent a number of years in prison and had also been a slave to alcohol. There was nothing dramatic about his conversion but the change that Christ has brought about over the course of time has given him a new sense of dignity and purpose for life. He knows his need to draw daily on the resources of God's grace through prayer and reading the Word of God. He has discovered, too, that the bond slave of Christ finds fulfilment in service and so gives voluntary help at a nearby Church Army hostel for the elderly.

Diakonos

Diakonos, on the other hand, is a functional word, stressing what we do for others rather than what we tell them to do for us. This is what is so astonishing about the attitude and actions of Jesus of Nazareth. From crib to grave his whole life was one of service. He gave himself in total obedience to the will of the Father and poured out his life in the service of mankind. His limitless compassion led him into one situation after another where there was need. He fed the physically and spiritually hungry. He healed the sick and gave sight to the blind. He restored hope and joy to the sorrowing. He opposed injustice and inequality. For Jesus it was service all the way.

It was service all the way for the Polish priest Fr. Maximilian Kolbe. In May 1941 he was arrested by the Nazis and sent to Auschwitz concentration camp where he received the striped convict garment and was branded with the number 16670. At every opportunity he spoke to the other inmates of the love of God and shared his meagre ration of soup or bread with those in special need. Once he was asked if such self-denial didn't amount to folly, but he answered, 'Every man has an aim in life. For most men it is to return home to their wives and families. For my part, I want to give my life for the good of all men.'

One day in July, a prisoner apparently escaped from Auschwitz, and camp authorities decided that ten men must die as a reprisal — starved to death in the dreaded windowless underground bunker. (In fact the 'escapee' was later found drowned in a camp latrine, so the terrible reprisals were quite unnecessary). The prisoners were paraded in the blazing midday sun and ten victims were selected at random. One of them, Franciszeck Gajowniczek, cried out in a despairing voice, 'My wife, my children, I shall never see them again.' To everyone's astonishment a man stepped out from the ranks and offered to take Gajowniczek's place. It was Maximilian Kolbe. The camp commandant agreed, so prisoner 16670 took the place of prisoner 5659 in the bunker. Not only did he help the other nine to die, but the inspiration of his presence brought comfort to others who were dying of hunger in cells near by. The cells resounded with hymns and prayers and the SS were astounded: *'So was haben wir nie gesehen'* (We never saw anything like it before), they said. Like his Master, Maximilian Kolbe laid down his life in the service of others.

No Status Seeking

Not surprisingly Jesus was never slow to challenge those who were concerned about position rather than about service. He had no time for status seekers.

Lesslie Newbigin describes a week he spent with a group of Pentecostal pastors in Chile, when he asked them what was the biggest problem that they faced in their Church. Immediately they answered with one Spanish word: *caudillismo* — bossism. Even in the setting of the Last Supper, the disciples were guilty of bossism.

... a dispute arose among them as to which of them was considered to be greatest. Jesus said to them, 'The kings of the Gentiles lord it over them; and those who exercise authority over them call themselves Benefactors. But you are not to be like that. Instead, the greatest among you should be like the youngest, and the one who rules like the one who serves. For who is greater, the one who is at the table or the one who serves? Is it not the one who is at the table? But I am among you as one who serves.'

(Luke 22:24–7)

It was during the Last Supper that Jesus gave his disciples an unforgettable lesson in service. John describes how Jesus 'got up from the meal, took off his outer clothing, and wrapped a towel round his waist. After that, he poured water into a basin and began to wash his disciples' feet, drying them with the towel that was wrapped round him' (13:4–5). The response from Peter was predictable: '... you shall never wash my feet ... Jesus answered, Unless I wash you, you have no part with me' (v.8).

The leader who would take the towel and serve others must first allow Jesus to get near enough to wash him clean from all grime of petty selfishness and self-importance. We talk much about what we do for God whereas true Christian service begins with the recognition and acceptance of what God, and God alone, has done for us in Christ. The feet-washing in the Upper Room was to find its consummation on the morrow when Jesus as the Suffering Servant, foreshadowed in Isaiah's four Servant Songs, made his final, complete act of obedient service on the Cross, bearing the sins of the world. To this there can be only one appropriate response:

> Nothing in my hand I bring.
> Simply to thy Cross I cling.
> Foul I to the fountain fly
> Wash me, Saviour, ere I die.[6]

The Christian leader has to keep close to the Cross, the place of forgiveness and limitless grace.

Those who would lead and point others to Christ must, in turn, take the towel and follow in the path of service. Such a path spells death to pride and to any ideas of leadership as an ego-trip. It will lead to misunderstanding and even ridicule. But Jesus's pattern of ministry must be our own. 'Now that I, your Lord and Teacher, have washed your feet, you also should wash one another's feet. I have set you an example that you should do as I have done for you . . .' (vv. 14–15).

There is little doubt that Simon Peter had the Upper Room picture of Jesus with the towel and basin carved for ever on his memory. In later years he was to urge his readers, 'Clothe yourselves with humility towards one another' (1 Pet. 5:5).

Love Through Service

In her work among the destitute and dying in the streets of Calcutta, Mother Teresa has become a legend in her own lifetime. Yet she, who is a world figure and who is the head of the Order of the Missionaries of Charity, leads by her own example of service, a service which still includes cleaning out the toilets in her community.

In addition to their work in Calcutta, the Missionaries of Charity have centres in other parts of the world. Mother Teresa describes an incident from Australia:

Some months back a man who had been beaten up was picked up from the streets of Melbourne. He was an alcoholic who had been for years in that state and the Sisters took him to their Home of Compassion. From the way they touched him and the way they took care of him, suddenly it was clear to him 'God loves me!' He left the Home and never touched alcohol again, but went back to his family, his children and his job. After, when he got his first salary, he came to the Sisters and gave them the money saying, 'I want you to be for others the love of God, as you have been to me.'[7]

What will it mean for us to 'be for others the love of God' and take the towel of service?

First, it will affect our attitude towards those we lead. We will see them, not as supporters who are there for our benefit to be used or even manipulated, but as brothers to be served in the name of Christ. Michael Green writes, 'It is no accident that the term "ministry" is used to describe the whole of Jesus's public life and work. He was supremely and in everything the Servant of the Lord. This was his glory; he looked for no other. And so it must be with any ministry which claims to be truly Christian.'

As leaders we will not ask of others anything we are not prepared to do ourselves – the leader must always be willing to get his hands dirty. 'Do nothing out of selfish ambition or vain conceit, but in humility consider others better than yourselves. Each of you should look not only to your own interests, but also to the interests of others. Your attitude should be the same as that of Christ Jesus: Who, being in the very nature God, did not consider equality with God something to be grasped, but made himself nothing, taking the very nature of a servant, being made in human likeness' (Phil. 2:3–7).

On one occasion a man who carried a knife, and was prone to violent bursts of temper and aggression, came to our home to take issue with me on a particular matter. My wife heard voices raised angrily in my study and made a hurried prayer for wisdom. Into her mind flashed the words 'Coffee and chocolate biscuits'. She quickly arranged an attractive tray and her arrival promptly defused a highly tense situation. It was an act of caring service underlying the value of the other person.

Second, it will be expressed in a desire to pray for those we lead. To pray for another is, in fact, the greatest act of loving service we can make on their behalf. Jesus knew this and, fully aware of Simon Peter's vulnerability, assured him, 'Satan has asked to sift you as wheat. But I have prayed for you, Simon, that your faith may not fail. And when you have turned back, strengthen your brothers' (Luke 22:31–2). Jesus continues to pray for those he has called to follow and serve him. The Christian leader is to follow his example in interceding for others by the hidden ministry of prayer.

Service is associated with activity, with doing. But the service of prayer is a ministry open to everyone, whatever the physical limitations may be. Those in the forefront of active Christian leadership rely far more than they ever realise on the faithful prayer support of others behind the scenes.

One day came a letter from someone I had met only once: 'This morning I have had a burden laid upon me to pray for you ...' These assurances of prayer are humbling. They come as a reminder that greater things are wrought by the power of prayer than anything else in the world.

Third, it will affect our ambitions for those we lead. We will want their highest good. We will want them to grow in Christian maturity and stature even if we are left in the shade in the process. John the Baptist had a number of outstanding leadership qualities in his own right but he was totally self-effacing when it came to his role in comparison to Jesus. 'He must become greater; I must become less' (John 3:30). There can be no greater satisfaction for a leader, as for a parent, than when those for whom we are responsible grow and develop in Christian maturity and even begin to forge ahead of us.

When a new member joins our Community at Lee Abbey they are given a copy of *Life Together* by Dietrich Bonhoeffer. In it they read, 'The Church does not need brilliant personalities but faithful servants of Jesus and the brethren. Not in the former but in the latter is the lack.'[8]

> O Thou who art the light of the minds
> that know Thee;
> The life of the souls that love Thee;
> And the strength of the wills that serve Thee:
> Help us so to know Thee
> that we may truly love Thee;
> So to love Thee that we may truly serve Thee,
> Whom to serve is perfect freedom.[9]

Chapter 4

RETREATING TO ADVANCE

'Beware of the barrenness of a busy life' is a warning that every leader must heed. Those who lead others need to ensure that their own lives are being continually refreshed from the springs of God's grace and love and are being kept in proper balance. Where the relationship with God is shallow, this soon becomes evident to others. Furthermore, the leader himself can experience an inner hollowness and a growing sense of desperation because spiritual resources have dried up. Few Christian leaders do not lead busy lives, but busyness need not lead to barrenness.

Jesus of Nazareth had enormous pressures on him during the three years of his public ministry. Yet he maintained a relationship with his Father that daily sustained and renewed him. Whether early in the morning or late in the evening, he made the time to withdraw in order to be alone with God and replenish his strength. He knew that he had to retreat in order to advance. If daily withdrawal was top priority with Jesus, it dare not be any less for his followers and especially for those who lead in his name.

If other people look to us for spiritual leadership, then space has to be created to be alone with God so that batteries can be recharged and direction given. It was the Quaker, John Edward Southall, who said, 'We cannot go through life strong and fresh on constant express trains; but we must have quiet hours, secret places of the Most High, times of waiting upon the Lord when we renew our strength and learn to mount up on wings as eagles, and then come back to run and not be weary, and to walk and not faint.'[10]

Space to be Still

'Be still, and know that I am God' (Ps. 46:10). Just to say those familiar words can begin the process of creating inner stillness. The frenetic pace of life has to be countered by the carving out of space just to be still in God's presence. It may be that we find the idea of being alone and quiet with God rather threatening. We may feel we can cope with God if we are with others, or if we are doing all the talking in prayer, but to be quiet is a different matter. Yet we have no need to be afraid. God is love and he longs only for our company and our undivided attention. Once the Curé D'Ars, a French saint of the eighteenth century, asked an old peasant what he was doing sitting for hours in the church, seemingly not even praying. The peasant replied, 'I look at him, he looks at me and we are happy together.'

Patience with ourselves is needed in learning to be still in God's presence. To begin with our minds are over-active and our rampant thoughts are like monkeys jumping from one bough of a tree to another. As we persevere, so we relax and sense the Spirit of God bringing peace and order to our bodies, minds, emotions and spirits.

In the stillness and solitude we can be utterly ourselves. We know that we can hide nothing from the piercing scrutiny of God. There can be no pretence or sham but only the sheer relief of being accepted and loved.

Space to be still enables the leader to keep his life and responsibilities in true perspective. Into the stillness comes the reminder that it is God who is at the centre of the universe, not ourselves. In the stillness the One whom we so often reduce to pigmy proportions is seen in all his awesome majesty, greatness and glory. Yet in the stillness we also become aware of God's tenderness and intimate personal concern for us as our Father. 'For this is what the high and lofty One says – he who lives for ever, whose name is holy: "I live in a high and holy place, but also with him who is contrite and lowly in spirit, to revive the spirit of the lowly and to revive the heart of the contrite"' (Isa. 57:15). The Most High God is also the Most Nigh God.

In the stillness of God's presence we can examine and reinforce not only our relationship with God but also with others. We can sense whether this action or that attitude was not in line with the will of God. We are able to assess whether or not our reactions to others or to certain situations have been strong or weak. Pride, fear or selfishness are ruthlessly exposed and we have the opportunity to repent and receive forgiveness. A clear sense of direction can be received and a course of action decided upon.

When two people are in love words are sometimes superfluous. Just to be together is sufficient. True silence is the speech of lovers. So it is that nothing delights the heart of God more than when we create the space to fill with him, valuing him for who he is. It is then that God is able to reveal more and more of the greatness of his love to us. Fr. Jerome wrote, 'The soul in its littleness looks upon God in his greatness and loves him; and God in his greatness looks upon the soul in its littleness and loves it.'

It is often useful to have a pen and paper ready at hand so that note can be taken of what God says to us in the stillness. There may be a fresh truth about God or about ourselves that we don't want to forget. There may be a wrong that we have caused that needs to be put right and forgiveness sought. God may want to give us a good prod to write a letter, make a call, or take a decision. Our stillness gives God the chance to speak and then it is for us to obey, 'Speak, Lord, for your servant is listening' (1 Sam. 3:9).

Space to Speak

Prayer involves both stillness and speaking. I began with stillness because the natural tendency is for us to do all the speaking and not allow God a word in edgeways. Those who have any position of responsibility in the life of a local church invariably have to do a lot of speaking and are, therefore, particularly prone to doing all the talking with God. But after the space to be still there needs to be space to speak. Space to tell God all that is in our hearts. 'Do not be anxious about anything, but in everything, by prayer and petition, with thanksgiving, present your requests to God' (Phil. 4:6).

One of the most impressive leaders in the Old Testament was Daniel. Carried off as a young man into exile in Babylon, Daniel showed integrity and qualities for leadership that were soon to be recognised. In the years that followed he was entrusted with immense responsibilities during the reigns of no less than five kings. The secret of his influence is to be found in the closeness of his relationship with God in prayer. Busy leader though he was, he was never too busy to pray. His communion with God was the constant source of Daniel's wisdom, strength and inner serenity.

The Book of Daniel contains a number of interesting insights into the content of Daniel's prayers. Whatever the circumstances, he was quick to express praise and thanksgiving to God. When God revealed King Nebuchadnezzar's dream and its interpretation to Daniel, he praised the God of heaven, 'I thank and praise you, O God of my fathers: You have given me wisdom and power, you have made known to me what we asked of you, you have made known to us the dream of the king' (2:23). Or see him later in the reign of Darius when he defies the edict of the king. 'Three times a day he got down on his knees and prayed, giving thanks to his God, just as he had done before' (6:10). Throughout all his trials and vicissitudes Daniel's steadfast confidence in the sovereignty and might of his God was expressed in worship and adoration. Likewise, the Christian leader who is not slow to offer praise and thanksgiving when speaking to God in prayer finds that the cares and pressures of leadership fall into proper perspective. God is far greater than our greatest problems.

Daniel, too, has much to say to us about the place and power of intercession when we speak to God in prayer. Watch him at prayer in chapter 9 when he turns to the Lord and pleads with him 'in prayer and petition, in fasting, and in sackcloth and ashes' (v. 3). Read the prayer that follows as he identifies himself with his nation, confesses its sin and begs for God's mercy and forgiveness. There is no trace of leadership superiority in Daniel's attitude and prayer. He accepts his part in the corporate sin of the nation and provides a pointer to all who would intercede for their nation and church.

Chapter 10 takes us into the mystery of prayer. Here we are reminded of the invisible and hostile forces operating against the purpose of God. As he prays, Daniel finds he is caught up in this conflict. To pray is to enter a battle and fight against the Devil and all the powers of darkness that seek to dehumanise and enslave. Intercessory prayer takes the battle into the enemy's camp and lifts high the Cross to proclaim the victory of Christ. Woe betide the Christian leader who ignores that 'our struggle is not against flesh and blood, but against the rulers, against the authorities, against the powers of this dark world and against the spiritual forces of evil in the heavenly realms' (Eph. 6:12). We are not on a picnic but in a battle for which we need to wear God's armour (vv. 13–18). We have our heads in the sand and leave unguarded those for whom we are responsible.

At the end of January 1982 a specially-trained Italian police squad freed the kidnapped American General James Dozier, who had been held captive for forty-two days by Red Brigade terrorists. General Dozier, described by his aides as a devout Protestant and regular church-goer, said after his dramatic release. 'The power of prayer works. I'm here today to tell you that it works and it had a large part to play in my being here with you today . . . I pray regularly myself but during the last six weeks I was on the receiving end of many prayers and where I was you could sure feel it.'

It has been said that 'helplessness is the first and the surest indication of a praying heart'. By creating space in our day to speak to God in prayer, we are acknowledging our helplessness and complete dependence upon him. Through praise, thanksgiving and intercession we learn to exchange our weakness for God's strength.

Space to Read

The Rule of the Taize Community in France contains the injunction: 'throughout your day let work and rest be quickened by the Word of God. In your life of prayer and meditation seek the command that God addresses to you, and put it into practice without delay. Therefore, read little, but ponder over it.'[11] The Christian needs to be continually nourished by the Word of God: unless the Christian leader is reading, reflecting upon and obeying God's Word, he has nothing to share with others. Paul reminds us: 'All Scripture is God-breathed and is useful for teaching, rebuking, correcting and training in righteousness, so that the man of God may be thoroughly equipped for every good work' (2 Tim. 3:16–17).

There are two approaches that help to make the Word of God part of us when we read and reflect upon it. First, as expressed in the Rule of Taize, 'read little, but ponder over it'. When Dietrich Bonhoeffer was principal of a theological seminary in Germany, he and his students followed a daily pattern of reading and reflecting upon one verse of scripture. When they were working through the Beatitudes (Matt. 5:1–12) they kept a corporate silence for half an hour each morning, covering one Beatitude each week. The value of this approach can be quickly recognised. For example, 'Blessed are the poor in spirit, for theirs is the kingdom of heaven' (v. 3) is a verse that contains a breadth of meaning and promise that can offer something to the maturest as well as to the youngest Christian. As we expose ourselves to God's truth in that verse so it becomes God's word to us personally to be claimed and a challenge to be accepted. In this simple way God's life-giving Word becomes part of us.

The second important approach to the scriptures is to read and study them. 'Do your best to present yourself to God as one approved, a workman who does not need to be ashamed and who correctly handles the word of truth' (2 Tim. 2:15). There are some walls on our Lee Abbey estate that are superb examples of the craft of stone-masonry. The design and choice of materials bear the mark of men who are experts in their trade and are highly skilled in the use of their tools. The chief tool of the Christian leader is the Bible. If we are to use it as God intends then we need to work at it in order to understand and apply its teaching. Some Christians never get down to any serious Bible study but rely on a sketchy and haphazard approach to reading a few verses here and there—and often their favourite ones—when they feel like it. There is no lack of Bible reading notes, commentaries and concordances to help us explore the treasures of this library of sixty-six books which comprise the Bible.

In these two approaches to reading the Word of God it is not a case of an 'either/or' choice, but of using both methods to equip us in God's service. The Holy Spirit, as both author and interpreter, comes to our aid to inform our minds and to warm our hearts.

In 'Space to Read' I have largely concentrated on reading the Word of God but the Christian leader should read as widely as possible. John Wesley had a passion for reading and most of it was done on horseback when he rode sometimes as far as ninety miles in a day. Books on science, history and medicine, as well as the spiritual classics, would be propped up on the pommel of his saddle and in this way he covered a prodigious amount of literature. Biographies and autobiographies provide fascinating insights and material for the Christian leader, who will also want to have a Bible in one hand and a newspaper in the other so that he is firmly rooted in the world God loves.

Space to Relax

Many a leader in the local church has become dull company and drained of all spiritual vitality because he never finds time to relax. Jesus is concerned about the whole of our lives. 'I have come that they may have life, and have it to the full' (John 10:10).

An early Church legend describes the aged Apostle John going out now and again to play with a flock of doves. The birds would flutter about him and settle from time to time on his shoulders and hands, while he talked to them as if they were his human friends. On one such occasion a hunter passed by and expressed his surprise that a man so pious as St. John would amuse himself by such an activity as this. St. John, pointing to the bow in the hunter's hand, asked him why he carried it with a loosened string. 'Because', said the hunter, 'it loses its strength unless it is given a chance to unbend.' The old Apostle, smiling, replied, 'If even a piece of wood needs to unbend to retain its usefulness, why should you be surprised that a servant of Christ should sometimes relax and so keep himself stronger for his work?'

Chapter 5

THE WAY OF HOLINESS

Jogging has gained a secure foothold as a popular British pastime. I'm not a jogging fanatic but it helps to combat the slackening of middle-aged muscles and generally makes me feel more alert. Some of my thinking for this chapter took shape while I was out jogging. 'The Way of Holiness' is about a leader's need for consistency of life that reflects the character of his Master.

The Indian philosopher, Barra Dada, brother of Rabindranath Tagore, once said, 'Jesus is ideal and wonderful but you Christians, you are not like him.' According to those who reported the incident, it was not said bitterly but sadly. Had those Christians, by their lack of love and inconsistent lives, put a stumbling-block in the path of the kindly old philosopher who might otherwise have become a Christian?

On the other hand, it was said of one missionary that 'he walks as he talks'. His life was all of one piece and Christ was seen in and through him. This was true, too, of a missionary by the name of Dr. Logan who worked in Japan. It was he who was instrumental in the conversion of Dr. Kagawa, who was to become a selfless leader in the service of Christ and his Kingdom. Years later, someone said to Dr. Kagawa, 'Do you know Dr. Logan?' Smilingly he replied, 'He was the first one who showed me the blueprint of love.'

Transparency

J. S. B. Monsell's hymn of exquisite beauty and yet uncomfortable challenge expresses the heart of true worship and witness:

O worship the Lord in the beauty of holiness,
Bow down before him, his glory proclaim;
With gold of obedience, and incense of lowliness,
Kneel and adore him: The Lord is his Name.[12]

Worship offered on Sunday by the gathered congregation must be matched by the quality of life offered by the scattered congregation on Monday. There needs to be a natural overspill from the worship of Sunday to affirming God's worthship in daily living, Monday to Saturday. Christians are called to reflect the character of a holy God.

Yet holiness is out of date — so it is said. In many people's minds holiness is associated with a strait-jacketed, kill-joy, puritanical drabness that has no beauty, attractiveness or strength about it. This kind of holiness is portrayed by the mother in *Whisky Galore* who kept her son, a teacher in his twenties, locked up in his room with a Bible on the Sabbath for daring to go against her wishes.

In contrast, true holiness possesses a compelling beauty, attractiveness and a quiet strength. The one question Lesslie Newbigin wanted to ask of all the younger Christians he met in Russia was, 'How is it that in a situation where the Church is absolutely forbidden to use any kind of public communication, where printing press, radio and public meetings are forbidden, where even parents are not allowed to teach religion to their children, the Church goes on winning converts?' The answer he received was, 'The attractive power of the holy life.'

It was in Antioch that 'the disciples were first called Christians' (Acts 11:26). Some commentators suggest that this was a derisory description. More likely, the Christians in Antioch bore a common likeness to the Jesus they loved and served. There was a consistency in what they said, what they did, and how they lived.

This kind of holiness is infectious. Others see it, feel it and catch some of it themselves. Those in positions of Christian leadership make their greatest mark, not primarily by what they say, but by what they are.

We have all met people whom we can only describe as 'Saints

of God, holy men and women'. It has not necessarily been their words but the sheer quality of their lives that has attracted our attention. They are so full of the Spirit of Jesus that we sense his presence when we are with them. They are usually very humble people who are unaware of the impact they make on others. Their Christ-likeness is a challenge to us to be unafraid to embrace God's call to 'be holy, because I am holy' (Lev. 11:44) and to 'Make every effort to live in peace with all men and to be holy; without holiness no-one will see the Lord' (Heb. 12:14).

When William Barclay was a student at Trinity College, Glasgow, one of his tutors was a man called A. J. Gossip. William Barclay describes him as someone who 'lived closer to God than any man I have ever known'. On one occasion A. J. Gossip described a week when pressure of all kinds made it difficult to prepare his Sunday sermon as thoroughly as he should have done. 'You know the stairs up to the pulpit in St. Matthew's?' he said. 'You know the bend on the stairs? Jesus Christ met me there. I saw him as clearly as I see you. He looked at the sermon in my hand. "Gossip," he said to me, "is this the best you could do for me this week?" ' Gossip went on, 'Thinking back over the busyness of that week, I could honestly say, "Yes, Lord, it is my best." And', said Gossip, 'Jesus Christ took that poor thing Sunday morning and in his hands it became a trumpet.' And somehow, William Barclay added, when you knew Gossip it seemed quite natural that he should meet and talk with Jesus.[13]

In one of his many magnificent prayers that have been woven into the fabric of his letters, Paul prays that his readers 'may be pure and blameless until the day of Christ, filled with the fruit of righteousness that comes through Jesus Christ – to the glory and praise of God' (Phil. 1:10–11). The Greek word that is translated 'pure' means literally 'sun-tested' or 'sun-judged'. The Apostle may well have had in his mind slipshod sculptors who would produce statues from blemished stone, filling the cracks with wax and painting them over. But eventually the sun would peel the paint, melt the wax and reveal the cleverly covered ugliness. Those who lead others must accept the challenge to be men and women of transparent character, free from sham and pretence.

> Not only in the words you say,
> not only in your deeds confessed,
> But in a most unconscious way
> is Christ expressed.
> Is it in a beautiful smile?
> A holy light upon your brow?
> Oh no! I felt His presence while
> you laughed just now.
> To me 'twas not the truths you taught,
> to you so clear, to me so dim,
> But when you came to us you brought
> a sense of Him.
> And from your eyes He beckons me
> and from your lips His love is shed,
> 'till I lose sight of you and see
> The Christ instead.

Step by Step

Jogging in North Devon presents many contrasts. The lanes are narrow and the hills steep. Like most people I find it easier to run downhill than up! There are two alternatives in running up a steep hill. Either to keep your eyes fixed on a point well ahead or to keep your eyes down and concentrate on the next step. I tend to choose the latter because I find it the best way of eventually reaching the top. Every now and then I look up and see how far I have got and either feel disappointed or encouraged.

Jogging uphill is rather like one aspect of following Christ and accepting his discipline over our lives. It is certainly true for those who have the privilege and responsibility of Christian leadership of any kind. The steady, unspectacular, hard slog of taking a step at a time in obedience to Christ is often what is required. We prove our love for Jesus by our obedience to His will and commandments. To say, "Lord, Lord" is not enough. Words have to be translated into action. 'Not everyone who says to me "Lord, Lord," will enter the kingdom of heaven, but only he who does the will of my Father who is in heaven' (Matt. 7:21). God turns a deaf ear to our claims upon his attention if we are not prepared to submit our wills to his direction. Obedience, like gold, is costly. The Christian leader who is soft with himself will crumble in the face of temptation and pressure. Those who lead others must know their own dependence upon the forgiveness and grace of God so that their lives reflect the growing mastery of Jesus upon them.

J. C. Ryle, a Bishop of Liverpool in the last century, wrote, 'This I do boldly and confidently say, that true holiness is a great reality. It is something in a person that can be seen and known and marked and felt by all around. It is light — if it exists, it will show itself. It is salt — if it exists, its savour will be perceived. It is a precious ointment — if it exists, its presence cannot be hid.'[14]

Into my mind comes the picture of a young housewife whose care and concern for others on a small housing estate made a profound impression on all who knew her. She opened her home for mothers and toddlers and in many other practical ways unconsciously conveyed the love of Jesus. To speak of Christ was as natural as breathing for her.

Such holiness reveals the beauty of Jesus Christ who was 'full of grace and truth' and who himself was obedient to the will of the Father.

The Spirit of Love

Those who covet a Christ-likeness which makes them a blessing to others and to the world, know their complete reliance upon the radically transforming power of the Holy Spirit. Human effort and co-operation are important but only the Spirit can produce the characteristics that reflect the love and control of Jesus. The exact opposites to the self-indulgent acts of our sinful nature are to be seen in the fruit of the Spirit — 'love, joy, peace, patience, kindness, goodness, faithfulness, gentleness and self-control' (Gal. 5:22–3).

It is the fruit on a tree that tells others what kind of tree it is. The fruits of the Spirit are the visible signs of the ever-deepening work of God in our lives. The fruit of love is pre-eminent. It is love that finds expression in practical ways in the other fruit. Paul expands on this further in the great hymn of love in 1 Corinthians 13:

> This love of which I speak is slow to lose patience — it looks for a way of being constructive. It is not possessive: it is neither anxious to impress nor does it cherish inflated ideas of its own importance.
> Love has good manners and does not pursue selfish advantage. It is not touchy. It does not compile statistics of evil or gloat over the wickedness of other people. On the contrary, it is glad with all good men when truth prevails.
> Love knows no limits to its endurance, no end to its trust, no fading of its hope: it can outlast anything. It is, in fact, the one thing that still stands when all else has fallen.
>
> (vv. 4–7, J. B. Phillips)

If we substitute the name of Jesus for the word 'love' we find a perfect picture of our Lord's character. Is this an impossible ideal to emulate? No — what is portrayed in Jesus can become a growing reality as we open our lives daily to be filled by the cleansing, renewing Spirit of God.

One of the labours of Hercules was to cleanse the stables of Augeas. In them Augeas had stabled 3,000 head of oxen for thirty years, without ever once cleaning them out. It was the task of Hercules to clear away this vast accumulation of filth. He did not even attempt to do it himself. He deflected the course of two rivers so that they flowed through the stables and their cleansing tide did what no human effort could have done.

The Holy Spirit provides us with a cleansing, renewing power far greater than our own. As we open our lives to the rivers of the Spirit, the impurities that soil our lives are swept away and the transforming love of Jesus takes their place.

The 'Way of Holiness', as Isaiah describes it (35:8), is a road to be travelled with unflagging resolution and reliance upon the Spirit. There are no short cuts.

Chapter 6

DECIDING WHO WE ARE

All Christian leadership needs to be exemplified by an attitude of service, not of domination (Mark 10:43–5). Nevertheless, there are different models of leadership with which every leader will find some kind of identification. Omnicompetence is rare in leadership and where it is found it usually means that other potential leaders never get a look in! Every leader needs to decide upon his particular leadership style and abilities and then ensure, where possible, that others with complementary gifts are allowed to play their full part.

Eddie Gibbs writes, 'A good leader must be prepared to extend the base of leadership by encouraging others to share their particular expertise for the good of the whole. We must be ready to welcome other people to work alongside us, who have abilities in specific areas greater than our own, without feeling personally threatened by their presence. Remember, the chain is as strong as its weakest link. So a team will break apart unless weak links are reinforced.'[15]

You may well be able to see yourself in one, or more, of the following examples of different models of leadership.

Protective Parent

Many older leaders see themselves in the role of the protective parent. It is a role which often brings added security and confidence to those for whom they have a responsibility. A retired farmer and his wife, who have been active in Christian work throughout their lives together, shared with delight and justifiable pride the fact they were now looked upon as 'elder statesmen'. They had discovered a new role in their church with its predominantly youthful membership. Many young people sought their wisdom and guidance.

The protective parent instinct can be seen in the Apostle Paul when he writes to Timothy, exhorting and encouraging him to follow his example. 'What you heard from me, keep as the pattern of sound teaching, with faith and love in Christ Jesus. Guard the good deposit that was entrusted to you – guard it with the help of the Holy Spirit who lives in us' (2 Tim. 1:13–14). Throughout both his letters to Timothy, Paul reveals a touching parental concern for his 'son in the faith'.

The leader who fits the protective parental model will have a deep personal concern for his church or group members. Each one will be the object of caring, expectant prayer and will be given every help possible in order to grow in confidence and spiritual maturity.

A leader, though, like the protective parent, has to guard against the twin dangers of coddling and cramping. Spiritual 'children' need to be given space to grow in Christ and develop their own identity. A parental likeness may be apparent in the offspring but it must not become a slavish copy of the parent.

The protective parent leader must avoid an authoritarianism that can lead either to discouragement or to an unhealthy dependence by others. Discipline is needed within any church family or group but there are great dangers in a style of leadership that seeks to direct and govern the lives of its members too tightly.

Understanding Friend

This is the model of leadership which underlines the importance of the 'one-to-one' relationship. It is the antithesis of the aloof, remote approach to leadership. The 'understanding friend' type of leader wants to know and be known by each person he leads. This style of leadership will have a special appeal to younger leaders who want to avoid any impression of detachment from those older than themselves and from their peers. But older leaders also adopt this attitude of understanding in order to inspire the confidence of others.

The disciple Andrew would probably have allied himself with this style of leadership. He was not a 'front man' like his brother Peter but rather quietly he got on with the job of getting alongside those he met. Was it not Andrew who befriended the small boy with his picnic lunch and then introduced him to his Master when a hungry crowd needed to be fed? (John 6:8–9). Was it not Andrew who, with Philip, introduced to Jesus some Greeks who had come up to Jerusalem for the Passover Feast? (John 12:20–22).

During his campaigns, Field-Marshal Montgomery adopted a very informal relationship with his men during his tours of their camps. He would stand on an old box or crate, gather the soldiers in a circle around him and speak to them man to man. There was little doubt who was the commander but Monty's troops felt they knew him as a friend who understood them completely. He left them in no doubt as to what he expected of them and was able to gain their full trust and loyalty.

Every model of Christian leadership has its weakness and those who see themselves as understanding friends need to be on the alert for the right moment to exert leadership. Every leader has to be prepared to face issues and tackle situations that may require a change of role from that of the understanding friend.

Efficient Manager

A not uncommon complaint against many churches and their leaders is the apparent disregard for efficient management. Some Christian leaders give the impression that efficiency is a word which must not be part of the vocabulary of a 'spiritual' ministry. Others resist the idea of efficient management out of sheer laziness. To do this is to dishonour the Lord, to whom the best we can offer is due, and to disown the obligation of responsible stewardship. Some leaders will have particular attitudes and skills which equip them for management but every Christian leader needs to be as efficient as possible within his own limitations. Other help can often be found to strengthen the efficiency and effectiveness of a local church.

One reason why efficient management and administration in a local church is important is because of the reliance upon voluntary, rather than paid, help for so many of the church's activities. For example, when a church has a large membership the co-ordination of gifts and ministries demands a high degree of sensitivity and care so that available resources are used as effectively as possible. While the appointment of an administrator may be an unwarranted luxury in many churches, it will be of enormous value in other, larger churches. Such an appointment may well release the minister to concentrate on other areas that need his attention and distinctive gifts.

The Christian leader who identifies with the leadership model of the efficient manager has to guard against becoming unapproachable. Efficient management can even be a form of escapism from becoming too deeply involved in the needs of others. The efficient manager has to retain a warm heart and a readiness always to subject efficiency to the controlling love of Christ. He who looks to leaders for wise stewardship of all that he entrusts to them rewards the efficiency that is motivated by obedient love rather than the submission of cold duty.

Tireless Pioneer

Some leaders will see themselves in this role. There will always be the need of Christian leaders who will be out ahead breaking new ground. This is the Christian leader who tends to be a 'loner' and who finds it claustrophobic when confined to the same situation for too long. The pioneer Christian leader will want to possess more and more territory for God and will not be afraid to take risks in the process. While others tend to be cautious, he will want to get on with things. Attempting great things for God, he will expect great things from God. The Christian Church owes much to its pioneers.

Philip had a pioneering spirit. We first meet him in Acts 6 when he is one of the seven men chosen to ensure that the Grecian Jewish widows are not overlooked in the daily distribution of food. Like the others he was 'known to be full of the Spirit and wisdom' (v. 3). But then, in Chapter 8, we find Philip proclaiming Christ in a Samarian city where there was great joy because of the power of his preaching and the miraculous signs that followed. Later in the same chapter, Philip the pioneer has changed direction again at the bidding of the Spirit and on a desert road he meets an important official in charge of all the treasury of Candace, queen of the Ethiopians. This encounter was to transform the Ethiopian's life and he returned to his own country as a disciple of Jesus.

The story of Philip is both an encouragement and a healthy corrective to the pioneering Christian leader who may be tempted to follow his own ideas rather than God's. God greatly used Philip because he was obedient to the leading of the Spirit. The tireless pioneer of the Gospel needs to be constantly alert and obedient to the direction of the same Spirit and to have the backing and check of others in leadership.

Fearless Revolutionary

The revolutionary and the pioneer are often kindred spirits. Both find it hard to sit still and stay in the same place for long. The revolutionary Christian leader is dissatisfied with the status quo. Where change is resisted or where complacency has a secure grip, then sometimes revolution is necessary. There are many local churches where only a spiritual revolution will prevent fossilisation. This is not change for change's sake but change that allows the possibility of new life, of resurrection out of decay and death. It is a revolution inspired by love.

The church in Laodicea came under the condemnation of the living Christ because of its marked complacency. 'Because you are lukewarm, neither hot nor cold — I am about to spit you out of my mouth. You say "I am rich; I have acquired wealth and do not need a thing." But you do not realise that you are wretched, pitiful, poor, blind and naked' (Rev. 3:16–17). A revolution of refining, purifying love was needed.

By the time she was eighteen Rosario Riveria was a militant communist. On a number of occasions Rosario met and worked with the famed revolutionary Che Guevara, who fired her with passion for her country and humanity. During her guerrilla activities Rosario was driven by hatred of the privileged classes and whoever stood in her way. She felt no remorse over the blood she spilled on her assignments. But then began a process of change in her life and, chiefly through the ministry of Luis Palau, she became a committed Christian. The love of Christ penetrated her heart, which previously had been rock-hard against God.

With her neighbours Rosario has improved the poor Lima suburb where they live, bringing electric light and a water system into the area. She is concerned for justice and equality. She also visits schools to speak to young people and show them how only Christ can satisfy humanity's deepest longings. Rosario is convinced that only God's love can revolutionise her country of Peru.

A revolution of love is needed in our own country and in many parts of the Church. Such a revolution must be spearheaded by Christian leaders who are unafraid to be revolutionaries of love.

Skilled Conductor

In my teenage years I had a great deal of fun playing the viola. On a number of occasions I attended an orchestral summer school in Sherborne, Dorset. Participants were divided into four different orchestras according to their ability. During the course of the week we practised hard in our orchestral sections and in full orchestra to prepare for the final concert, which was always the highlight. The key person in the orchestra was, of course, the conductor. The conductor's ability to draw out the best from each player and section never ceased to amaze me. Somehow he helped us to stretch our capacities far beyond the point we believed possible. He skilfully drew together all the resources available and the final result brought immense satisfaction to the players and, dare I say it, considerable pleasure to the audience!

The skilled conductor has much to commend him as a model for Christian leadership in the local church. With its diverse membership and groups each church requires leadership that has the ability to draw out the fullest potential available. Christian leaders, like conductors, have to know what they want from others. They need to listen to the music of the Spirit, which then has to be interpreted to members, so that in turn they can respond and experience the joy of achievement. Like the sensitive conductor, Christian leaders will be eager to create a right blend of all the gifts and ministries. Even the tiniest congregations have possibilities that can be tapped and used. Above all, Christian leadership will want to encourage everyone to believe that God 'is able to do immeasurably more than all we ask or imagine, according to his power that is at work within us . . .' (Eph. 3:20).

Jean Vanier, founder of the L'Arche Communities for the handicapped, writes, 'A community is like an orchestra; each instrument is beautiful when it plays alone, but when they all play together, each given its own weight in turn, the result is even more beautiful.'[16]

What is true for a community is also true for a church.

Chapter 7

LEARNING AS WE GO

Most of the lasting lessons on leadership are learnt on the job. No amount of theory can be an adequate substitute for actually putting things into practice. People respond to challenge and mature with responsibility. In the classroom, tasks involving responsibility and leadership may seem beyond our capabilities but unrecognised capacity is discovered in the process of learning as we go.

It is intriguing and illuminating to see how Jesus set about training his disciples. Jesus trained the disciples by doing things, by meeting situations and then coming back and talking about them. The parables, which to many people were a complete mystery and had the over-all effect of puzzling the crowds, were explained to the disciples — but only after they had had time to think about them for themselves (e.g. the Parable of the Sower, Mark 4:1–20). An essential part of any training of people for leadership and responsibility has to be to help them work things out for themselves with the risk that sometimes they will come up with the wrong answers. Yet Jesus was prepared to take these risks and to trust his friends, the disciples, to share in his work.

Mark tells us that when Jesus chose the apostles, 'He appointed twelve ... that they might be with him and that he might send them out to preach and to have authority to drive out demons' (3:14–15). In having them 'with him' Jesus's aim was to train them by personal coaching. His approach was essentially practical. So it was that the streets, bazaars, fields, lake and the Temple were all used as arenas for schooling his followers for future leadership.

Theory has to be translated into real working situations.

Learning as We Go

Watching and listening are important but even more vital is the actual 'doing'. For example, the coach of a football team may show a video recording of a previous game. Tactics are analysed and strengths and weaknesses noted. But what really counts is the action that will take place in the next game when lessons learnt have to be applied.

Jesus not only wanted the apostles to be 'with him' but also 'that he might send them out ...' It was in the going that they were to discover just how much they could accomplish with his commission and power.

Sink or Swim

Ordination for an Anglican minister is followed by a period of several years as curate. This is largely intended as the next stage in the training received at theological college.

My curacy, in the town church of Christ Church, Woking, was with the Revd. Eric Hague. Eric and Greta Hague had served in China with the Church Missionary Society for a number of years. No task or sacrifice was ever too great in their care of people in the parish. Eric had a disturbing habit of sometimes asking me to do something without any prior warning. Agonising though this could be, his 'sink or swim' method usually worked. It taught me some invaluable lessons of adaptability and resourcefulness in leadership during those formative years. I've not been unknown for using the same method with others! Only by having to do something do we actually realise that we can do it in the strength of a God who delights to astonish us by matching his power to our weakness.

It is not difficult to picture the exhilaration of the 'seventy-two' after their return to Jesus (Luke 10). We don't know how long most of them had been with him but probably not for long. Jesus, though, judged that the time was ripe for them to take their leadership training course a stage further. He sent them 'two by two ahead of him to every town and place where he was about to go' (v. 1). He didn't mince his words but gave them clear instructions and warned them of the dangers ahead.

'Go! I am sending you out like lambs among wolves' (v. 3). So off they went with their knees knocking and their hearts pounding. They must have been scared stiff.

What a transformation when they returned! They recounted the stories of how they had experienced God's power at work in the lives of many they met. With undisguised amazement they said, 'Lord, even the demons submit to us in your name' (v. 17). The lessons they had learnt as messengers of the Kingdom of God were to prove invaluable in the years ahead when the leadership of the early Church was to fall upon their shoulders.

When teams return to Lee Abbey after leading a mission or conducting a training programme in different parts of the country, they report back to the rest of the Community. The atmosphere is not unlike the return of the seventy-two as they describe what God has done through them and, often, in spite of them. Some will have had to lead and speak at home meetings, others to take part in music and drama events in schools, colleges or in the street. All will have had to bear witness to their faith in Christ and in the process sometimes face hard questioning and antagonism. In these 'front line' situations faith and trust in the Living God is deepened and toughened.

One Community member described how she felt when asked to speak to a large gathering of people.

Humanly speaking, I was terrified to get up and share my own faith in Christ with people of such different experiences in life from my own. But the Holy Spirit took me in my nervousness and took my words in their simplicity and used them for his purposes. It was one of a number of concrete examples of God's presence in my life and of how he fulfils his promises.

Spiritual Saturation

Too much Christian teaching is not put into action. Just as there is an abysmal lack of teaching in many churches so that members are unable to give an informed and coherent 'reason for the hope that is in them', in other churches the congregations suffer from a surfeit of teaching. Sleek and sluggish, they sit there like young cuckoos, demanding more and more. Spiritual saturation is by no means a rarity. It is remedied not by more teaching, but by action. The well-taught Christian and the well-taught congregation have an inescapable obligation to put what they have received into practice. The privilege of having been given much brings with it the responsibility to share much with others. 'Learning as we go' allows this to happen.

Where members of a congregation do begin to develop a concern for the wider community and start to explore different ways of sharing Christ's love with others, a fresh sense of purpose can be discovered. What has been assimilated over the years is no longer jealously guarded, but released. Leaders should provide the impetus for this to happen.

Bumps and Bruises

'Learning as we go' can be far from straightforward. There will be times of failure as well as success. Jesus was prepared for this to happen as he brought his disciples into his confidence and shared his ministry with them.

There was the incident involving the disciples and a boy who had an evil spirit (Mark 9:14–29). The boy's father had taken the child to the disciples and asked them to drive out the spirit but they were unable to do so. Jesus's authority over the evil forces that dehumanise proved decisive and the boy was restored to full health. Afterwards, the disciples asked Jesus privately why they hadn't been able to deliver the boy. 'This kind can come out only by prayer', was Jesus's reply. Another lesson had been learnt, but this time through failure rather than success. We learn most of our unforgettable lessons through failure.

John Mark discovered that failure was an important lesson in the school of leadership. The apostle Paul had spotted his potential and he and Barnabas had taken Mark with them on their first missionary journey. We don't know the reasons but at Pamphylia Mark had deserted them and when Barnabas later wanted to give Mark another chance, Paul was not prepared to take the risk. Their sharp disagreement caused them to part company, with Barnabas taking Mark and sailing for Cyprus and Paul and Silas going through Syria and Cilicia. But in later years, Paul was to acknowledge that Mark's failure did not exempt him from again having an effective ministry. 'Get Mark, and bring him with you because he is helpful to me in my ministry' was his instruction to Timothy (2 Tim. 4:11).

There is a garage in Buckinghamshire which carries a large notice bearing the words 'M.O.T. FAILURES WELCOMED'. It's an invitation that brings hope to the motorist whose car has failed to pass the Ministry of Transport requirements! The carpenter of Nazareth is an expert in mending and making new lives that have been marred through failure. For the leader, he takes the failures and creates something of greater strength and usefulness out of them.

Bumps and bruises come not only through failure but also from facing difficulty. Yet it is in facing and overcoming difficulties that training and experience in leadership are strengthened. When writing to the leaders and members of the Church in Thessalonica, Paul thanks God for 'your work produced by faith, your labour prompted by love, and your endurance inspired by hope in our Lord Jesus Christ' (1 Thess. 1:3). Here were Christians who welcomed the message of the Gospel with great joy and then put it into practice in spite of severe suffering (v. 6). Consequently, they 'became a model to all the believers in Macedonia and Achaia' (v. 7). It is often through suffering and difficulty that steel is given to our faith and lessons are learnt in leadership that prove of incalculable worth.

The story is told of a man who began a study of butterflies. Two cocoons of an extraordinarily beautiful specimen were placed where the spring sun would shine on them. Under the warmth a curious shell began to swell. One, a little in advance of the other, broke open and a butterfly appeared. Since this variety of butterfly was famed for the splendour of its colours he was perplexed by the fact that the little creature's wings were drab. As it struggled to work itself free of the shell, he observed that it was being held by a tiny white cord. With his knife he cut the thread and liberated the fragile struggler. It flew about the room; but to his dismay there was no sign of glorious colour.

With the second cocoon he decided to let nature take its course. There was the same initial struggle, the same slender thread, the same seeming frustration on the part of the new-born insect. For more than an hour the little creature fought for its freedom. Even before the struggle was over, the colour began shooting out into its wings, and when at last the battle was won, those wings were simply glorious.

This parable from nature is a reminder that Christian maturity in living and leadership develops, like the Thessalonian Christians, through 'endurance' in the face of difficulty and suffering. Butterflies that mature without battle mature without beauty. Is it not true that many of the leaders that God has greatly used in the Christian Church in the course of history have borne the battle scars of suffering which in turn have produced a compelling beauty of character?

'Learning as we go' is often a painful and humbling process, but the marks that remain will inspire greater confidence from others in our leadership.

Vulnerability

The leader who never reveals his own vulnerability but keeps a protective cover over himself will never be able to help others to develop in leadership. Jesus allowed his disciples not only to see him in all his glory on the Mount of Transfiguration but also to see both his strengths and his vulnerability in the Garden of Gethsemane. They witnessed him in his agony when, broken, bleeding and accursed, he was crucified on a Roman gibbet at Calvary. 'And being found in appearance as a man, he humbled himself and became obedient to death — even death on a cross!' (Phil. 2:8). Here is the summit of vulnerability — the Son of God accepting to the full the cost of exposing his heart of love to the world he had come to redeem.

How far do we share ourselves with others as leaders? It can, of course, be unhelpful and even unhealthy to share some experiences with others, but there will be many occasions when openness about failure and difficulty, as well as success, can allow other people more intimately into our lives. Those wanting to learn how to lead find it impossible to identify with a leader who sets himself apart. The youngest beginner in the school of Christian leadership relates at once to the experienced leader who is able to share both set-backs and success, frustration and fulfilment.

The leader who masks his vulnerability, perhaps out of fear caused by past hurts or rejection, can become remote and unreachable. When we are prepared to be vulnerable and open to others, we are saying that we want to go on learning in the school of leadership. This school lasts a lifetime.

Chapter 8

SPOTTING THE POTENTIAL

It has been said that leaders are born, not made; but I believe that more leaders are made than were ever born. Leadership is largely a matter of training. It is a relative matter; capacity grows with experience as the qualities of leadership are discovered and developed.

Golda Meir, for example, was the daughter of an impoverished carpenter. With great determination she developed leadership qualities that equipped her to be an outstanding prime minister of Israel at a point in her life when most people would have opted for retirement.

What an extraordinary woman Golda Meir was!

There were many days in the spring and summer of 1973, when I fell into bed at two in the morning and lay there, telling myself that I was crazy. At seventy-five I was working longer hours than I had ever worked before and travelling more, both inside Israel and abroad, than was good for anyone. Although I really did my best to cut down on appointments and delegate more work, it was much too late for me to turn into another person.[17]

The Call of Jeremiah

Many centuries before Golda Meir another great patriot had a leading role to play in the history of Israel. It was also a lonely role and one which brought great heartache and suffering. Jeremiah was called by God to proclaim judgment on an unresponsive, apostate nation. Despite the sombreness of the word he had to deliver, he does not deserve to be known only as a prophet of woe. He was also a prophet of hope in the midst of catastrophe.

Neither Jeremiah nor his contemporaries recognised his potential for leadership. Though he was a priest by birth and came from an influential family, there was no early indication of the prophetic function he was later to exercise. Jeremiah's main concern was to keep out of the limelight. But God had other plans.

> 'Before I formed you in the
>   womb I knew you,
> before you were born
>   I set you apart;
> I appointed you
>   as a prophet to the nations.'
>   (Jer. 1:5)

All Jeremiah's protestations were of no avail. God had seen beyond what he was to what he could become. The potential was there and, furnished with anointing power, Jeremiah began his ministry as a mouthpiece of the Lord.

You are : You will Be

When we read the Gospel we see how Jesus was always quick to spot the potential in other people. 'You are Simon son of John. You will be called Cephas' (John 1:42). Bishop John Taylor writes, ' "You are: You will be" — the actual and the potential. Both must be seen equally clearly and both must be seen together. For when the truth of the other confronts the truth of myself it demands that I be myself, but also that I be all that I'm capable of being.'[18] Jesus could see that Peter, the man of sand, would one day become the man of rock. Through training and testing, failure and forgiveness, the unreliable, impetuous Peter would become a strong, dependable and wise leader of the Church in Jerusalem.

A big lump of something — a stone supposedly — lay for

centuries in a shallow brook in North Carolina. Passers-by saw only an ugly lump and passed on. One day a poor man stopped by the brook and spotting the heavy lump decided to take it home to use to keep his front door ajar. Months later a geologist was passing his house and stopped in amazement when he saw the large door-stop. It was a lump of gold, the biggest ever found east of the Rockies!

Jesus spotted the gold in Simon Peter. He also saw the gold in John, another of the fishing fraternity. It was John who later was to write:

> Dear friends, let us love one another, for love comes from God. Everyone who loves has been born of God and knows God ... since God so loved us, we also ought to love one another. No-one has ever seen God; but if we love each other, God lives in us and his love is made complete in us
>
> (1 John 4: vv. 7, 11, 12)

Could this be the same man, writing with such tenderness, who had urged Jesus to call fire down from heaven to consume a Samaritan village? Yes, but Jesus knew that John, the son of thunder, would one day become an apostle of love, refined like gold by the fire of the Spirit.

The Christian Church owes an incalculable debt to the apostle Paul and his outstanding qualities of leadership. But who spotted his potential — a potential that could have so easily been wasted? Barnabas — is the answer. On two occasions he gave Paul the vital break that he needed. First, he ensured his acceptance by the church leaders in Jerusalem. Understandably, they were afraid of this former arch-enemy of the Church. Barnabas was able to allay their fears and convince them that Paul's conversion was genuine. From then on he could move around freely, 'speaking boldly in the name of the Lord' (Acts 9:28).

Paul's second big break came when Barnabas was sent down to Antioch to assess the situation after a great many people had responded gladly to the preaching of the good news. Barnabas soon realised that what was urgently needed were the teaching and leadership gifts of Paul. He went to Tarsus to find him and brought him back to Antioch. 'For a whole year Barnabas and Saul met with the church and taught great numbers of people. The disciples were first called Christians in Antioch' (Acts 11:26).

From this point Paul never looked back. His potential as a leader and teacher had been spotted and allowed to blossom by Barnabas. No wonder the disciples nicknamed him 'the son of encouragement'. He was always eager to help others develop their full potential.

Feeling Secure

One of the most important priorities for any minister is to spot and develop the potential for leadership of those within the congregation. In order to do this he must feel secure in his own personal sense of call and his own responsibility in the overseeing of the church. If he feels insecure the last thing he will want to do is to open his ministry in such a way that others have the opportunity to fulfill their own potential for leadership. He will be afraid of others who might challenge, surpass or just ignore him. The insecure minister will generally play safe by keeping as much power as possible in his own hands or in the hands of 'yes-men'.

Sadly, this form of insecurity is still widespread in spite of all the significant developments in local church leadership. This lack of a clear sense of security amongst many ministers is an adverse reflection on the kind of preparation for leadership and 'man-management' received at theological college. In Charles Davis's apologia for leaving the Roman Catholic Church he had some hard things to say about the clerical imprisonment the Church has built for itself:

> The making of the Christian Minister into a priestly class, set apart and possessing a priesthood different in kind from the rest of Christians, disrupted the Christian community. It led to the degradation of the laity, the obscuring of the nature of Christian life and mission, the distortion of the

Christian liturgy to hieratic ritual and its eventual fossilisation.[19]

Charles Davis's words of condemnation could be applied equally to other parts of the Christian Church. But it would be only fair to say that many more colleges and non-residential courses preparing men and women for ordination and other forms of ministry, are now far more realistic in their training programmes for Christian leadership. Gradually the effects of this will percolate into the strategic thinking of how best to spot, develop and use lay leadership in the life of the local church.

Out of the Freezer

Freezers are a modern invention for which many a housewife has cause to be grateful. Food is kept by being frozen and then, when needed, it is taken out, heated and presented at a meal months later. But the purpose of the freezer would be wasted if the food remained stored in it for too long, or if it were taken out and offered half-frozen at dinner. Yet this illustrates precisely what still happens in far too many churches. God's people are either kept in cold storage or, at best, are half-frozen because they have never been used to their full potential.

Paul's favourite metaphor of the church as 'the body of Christ' leaves us in little doubt that there are to be no frozen or sleeping partners. 'Just as each one of us has one body with many members, and these members do not all have the same function, so in Christ we who are many form one body, and each member belongs to all the others' (Romans 12:4-5).

The human body is a living, vital organism with its constituent parts all knowing that they belong to the rest of the body and have their own valued and distinctive role to play. Where a church has been warmed by the love of Christ and is open to the life-giving Spirit, its members know that they belong to a living, worshipping, witnessing body of people. They know that they count and that God has given to them gifts and ministries to be used for the benefit of everyone. In such an environment of expectancy and mutual care, gifts that relate to leadership can be discovered, trained and used.

The minister who is eager to develop lay leadership in the church should be constantly on the alert. Like Sherlock Holmes he will be doing his own detective work in spotting and encouraging the development of leadership potential in the congregation. 'Who takes the lead when people are together?' 'Whose opinion is listened to with care and respect in a committee or in a group discussion?' 'Who puts forward ideas that are adopted?' 'Who has the ability to get alongside other people and make them feel that they matter?' Above all, 'Who reveals a growing commitment to the Lordship of Christ that clearly affects their priorities and general attitude?' In these and other ways the minister will gradually build up a picture of the kind of leaders that God has 'up his sleeve' for positions of responsibility, either immediately or at some point in the future. It's rather like putting together the pieces of a jigsaw puzzle, searching for the right person for the right place.

Be Warned

Ministers, in particular, need to beware of the 'pigeon-hole' mentality. This is the mentality that works like this: 'Ah, Mr W. works in a bank. He is just the man we need as treasurer of the new hall appeal fund. Then there is Mrs T. She trained as a teacher and will be ideal in the Sunday School.' Mr W. may well be happy to become the treasurer of the new hall appeal fund and Mrs T. may be willing to join the teaching team at the Sunday School. On the other hand, both may be longing for other latent gifts to be developed and would feel a far greater sense of fulfilment if they were encouraged to offer themselves for other areas of service and leadership in the life of the church.

It's much safer to 'pigeon-hole' people for positions of responsibility but far more risks need to be taken with people whose potential for leadership may be considerably greater than is realised.

Another warning. There will always be some people for

whom a position of leadership in the church offers an opportunity to satisfy an innate urge to exercise power over others. Inevitably, their number will include some who are frustrated in their jobs or who are unfulfilled in their relationships. One readily and thankfully acknowledges that belonging to the church of Jesus Christ opens up new horizons for personal growth through service for many whose lives would otherwise be unsatisfied, but there will always be those whose motives for seeking a place of influence will be suspect. Many a church rues the day when the responsibilities for one of its activities or groups came under the iron grip of a power-hungry leader.

How important, therefore, that the minister and those with whom leadership may be shared should ensure that every position of responsibility in the church is filled with much care and prayer. Better not to fill a gap than to take the risk of appointing someone about whom we might have reservations. If, for example, the leadership of the youth group or the chairmanship of a committee is in the wrong hands, the consequences are sooner or later felt by other parts of the church. The spiritual vitality of the church is sapped by internal tensions in leadership.

Time Well Spent

I'm always impressed by the priority that Jesus gave in his time and teaching to the small group of twelve men whom he had chosen to be with him. He who had assessed their potential and knew their weaknesses as well as their strengths, was fully aware that his time with them was short. Three years would soon be over and then they would be thrust to the forefront of leadership. His strategy of concentrating increasingly on the training of the disciples rather than on speaking to the crowds was to be fully vindicated.

Time spent in spotting and developing gifts for leadership will always be time well spent. Moreover, it ensures that the leadership of the local church is not dominated by one person but undergirded by others sharing responsibility at every level.

Chapter 9

REACHING MEN

'What can the Church offer that will attract successful business-men to its ranks?' My questioner, a highly resourceful and prosperous business-man, went on to illustrate his point with uncomfortable forcefulness.

Whenever the subject of men and the Church is raised the reactions of local church leaders are predictable. There are those who will retort — sometimes even smugly — that their church membership contains a sizeable number of men. In contrast, other leaders will reply that men are notable by their absence from their congregation. They feel a sense of failure and are perplexed as to how to remedy the situation.

The plain fact is that the Church very largely fails to attract men into its company and, where men are to be found in the local church, they are rarely motivated and used to their full capacity. It is for this reason that reaching and motivating men must figure prominently in the strategy of local church leader-ship.

Jesus and Men

The impact of Jesus of Nazareth upon men was extraordinary. The Gospel records leave us in little doubt that Jesus made a profound impression upon men and a number were prepared to give him their total allegiance, leaving everything to follow him. What a motley crew they were! They included tough fishermen like Peter and Andrew, James and John, a devious tax collector called Matthew, and Simon, a revolutionary. It is hard to imagine the 'gentle Jesus, meek and mild' figure portrayed so often by the artist as the same Jesus who was able to command the respect and devotion of men from such diverse backgrounds. Nor was the compelling attraction of Jesus only felt by men during his lifetime. Saul of Tarsus, an intellectual, and Luke, a cultured physician, were prepared to go anywhere and do anything in obedience to the will of Christ. There was certainly no shortage of men in the early Church.

What can we learn, then, from Jesus and his early followers about how to reach and motivate men in the service of Christ today?

Risk-Takers

The men who followed Jesus and who were later to be at the hub of the leadership in the early Church, were attracted by a strong element of risk. For example, the call of Levi (Matthew) comes as a startlingly direct challenge to take a huge risk. 'As he walked along, he saw Levi son of Alphaeus sitting at the tax collector's booth. "Follow me," Jesus told him, and Levi got up and followed him' (Mark 2:14). From the comparative security of a lucrative profession, Levi was prepared to take the plunge of leaving everything behind and joining forces with Jesus of Nazareth for an unknown future.

Dietrich Bonhoeffer writes: 'When we are called to follow Christ we are summoned to an exclusive attachment to his person. The disciple simply burns his boats and goes ahead ... He is called out, and has to forsake his old life in order that he may "exist" in the strictest sense of the word. The old life is left behind, and completely surrendered ... Beside Jesus nothing has any significance. He alone matters.'[20]

To follow Christ is to join the company of risk-takers. To be willing for whatever Jesus requires of us. To do what he asks, and go where he directs. To be prepared not to know what will follow beyond the first all-important step of obedience. Many men are outside the Church because they see no evidence of risk and adventure within it. The members seem dull and the programme and activities appear tame. There is little or nothing that evokes interest and arouses curiosity. If the element of risk and adventure was evident in our churches, more men would be asking, 'What am I missing? What's the secret? Where can I fit in?'

There is always the danger of trying to translate a first century situation into the twentieth century. Yet J. B. Phillips's challenge is unavoidable:

> The reader is stirred because he has seen Christianity, the real thing, in action for the first time in human history. The new-born Church, as vulnerable as any human child, having neither money and influence nor power in the ordinary sense, is setting forth joyfully and courageously to win the pagan world for God through Christ. The young Church, like all young creatures, is appealing in its simplicity and single-heartedness. Here we are seeing the Church in its first youth, valiant and unspoiled — a body of ordinary men and women joined in an unconquerable fellowship never before seen on this earth.
>
> Yet, we cannot help feeling disturbed as well as moved, for this surely is the Church as it was meant to be.[21]

Men sit up and take notice when their local church is obviously not prepared to play safe. Their respect may be won when those who gather for worship on Sundays translate their faith into their attitudes and actions from Monday to Saturday. When it is evident that being a Christian gives direction and purpose to life, then men will often want to know more. The call of Levi has an interesting sequel, as Mark records: 'While Jesus was having dinner at Levi's house, many tax collectors and "sinners" were eating with him ... for there were many who followed him' (2:15). Predictably, the Pharisees were aghast at the risks he took. But the safety of the synagogue or the company of only religious people held no attraction for Jesus. He always wanted to be where people needed him most and where the good news of the Kingdom would be received gladly and hungrily.

Reaching Men

On December 12th, 1980, Ridley Hall Evangelical Church in Battersea, South London, completed the purchase of the bakery next door. The church's annual income at the time of the purchase was only about £2,000. Yet the small congregation believed that God wanted them to take risks and tackle a project that would involve transforming the bakery into a homely centre for expressing the love of Christ in the area. A total of £6,000 was given in gifts and £24,000 was raised by loans and the bakery became theirs. Church members worked to the point of exhaustion, plumbing, plastering, renovating windows and doors, decorating and fitting gas appliances.

April 27th, 1981, was the day for the opening and dedication of the newly acquired and renovated premises. A comfortable lounge, counselling room, kitchen and soon a play-school and 'latchkey kids' centre were all included in the premises. In addition, the old bakery provides accommodation for six young people in the congregation who now form a small, informal Christian community bearing witness to Jesus by the quality of their life together and by their caring for others in the neighbourhood. Not surprisingly, this venture of faith is steadily attracting others, including men, to join this company of risk-takers.

Clear Objectives

If men are attracted by the element of risk, they also respond to clear objectives. Many men work in situations where the objectives of their company or firm are clearly defined. These objectives provide incentives for achievement and success, pride of performance and job fulfilment. At the beginning and at the end of Matthew's Gospel, Jesus plainly states his objectives. 'Come, follow me, and I will make you fishers of men' was his invitation to Simon Peter and Andrew (4:19). 'Go and make disciples of all nations' was the command of the risen Christ to the eleven disciples in Galilee (28:19). Here were objectives that were unambiguous in their directness and awesome in their implications.

At one stage I was involved with a small group in clarifying the 'purpose, aims and objectives' of the Diocese of St. Albans. As an exercise it was intended to help stimulate congregations to look at themselves more honestly and to clarify their objectives. Far too many churches and Christian groups drift on aimlessly from month to month, year to year, without any clear sense of direction. To do so is irresponsible and can be spiritually disastrous. It is not sufficient to say, 'Our only objective is to obey the leading of the Spirit.' Jesus described the Holy Spirit as 'Another Counsellor to be with you for ever' (John 14:16). Part of the Spirit's role is to come alongside God's people and help them hammer out clear objectives that will bear his stamp of approval upon them. Yes, of course, we must also be willing to change direction at any point if the Holy Spirit indicates, but the clarifying of objectives is a necessary part of responsible leadership. To carry this further, each group and organisation within a local church needs to decide the objectives that it will seek to fulfil over a period of time. A one-year, three-year or five-year plan is not to be despised. Rather, it is evidence of a prayerfully and responsibly thought-out strategy which may arouse men's interest and encourage their involvement.

'MISSION REACHES TOWN'S YOUTH' was a front page headline in the *Berkhamsted Gazette* following an ecumenical mission in March 1982, led by a Lee Abbey team and involving all the churches in the town. As part of the mission young people in the area and all the schools were visited by team members who used music and drama to convey the good news of Christ. Each evening the Court House, renamed 'The Way Inn', was packed with teenagers. Interest in 'The Way Inn' had grown throughout the week to a point where young people were arriving an hour before the doors opened. Others who arrived with half an hour to spare didn't get in at all! It was significant that those who had shared in the planning of the evening youth events had set a number of clear objectives for the week: an average of seventy young people a night; twenty-five to become Christians as a result of the week's programme; fifty to become integrated into the regular activities of the church youth groups in the town. These objectives provided targets for expectant prayer and they were soon to be surpassed. The youth work in the town has taken on a new sense of purpose and vitality.

If you are involved in the leadership of a church or group, have any objectives been shaped? If not, it may be right to work out your own simple 'purpose, aims and objectives' exercise and then apply it. To do so would give fresh impetus and enthusiasm for the work for which you have a responsibility. Moreover, others will sense that here is a church or a group that knows where it is going. Examples of local church objectives may read like this:

1. Increase church membership by 10% annually.
2. Create a link with an overseas or inner-city project that will widen horizons.
3. Visit every home in the area within the next three years and prepare a number of visiting teams to accomplish the task.
4. Increase church magazine/newsletter circulation from 300 to 500 during the next two years.
5. Within the next six months open up three new Home Groups.
6. Initiate four events over the next two years which will aim to draw together the other churches in the area.

It can be very helpful and healthy for a church to assess its objectives at regular intervals. In the process it may well be discovered that some organisations, activities and committees are no longer playing a necessary part in the life of the church. They may, in fact, be a detrimental factor and draining the energies of church members, thereby hampering the possibility of a new work beginning in obedience to the Spirit. This is where leadership in the local church sometimes requires courage to use the pruning knife so that the dead wood can be cut away and something new can grow. 'As it was in the beginning, is now and ever shall be' is an attitude entirely out of context when applied to many groups and activities still in existence in the Church today!

Men outside the Church of Christ will, I believe, take more

notice when they see evidence of risks being taken and clear objectives stated and pursued. They will also be interested to see what use is made of the men who are already part of the local church. What happens to the men we have already got?

Wasted Manpower

A cursory look around many churches today will reveal a crisis situation of mass unemployment, or at the least, mis-employment. Men, generally speaking, are given jobs like cutting the grass in the churchyard, pulling the bell, taking and counting the collection, reading a lesson, clearing up after the jumble sale and offering transport to church or hospital. None of these tasks is unimportant and all need to be done and done well. Yet if these are the only jobs that the local church can offer it is no wonder that many soon feel frustrated. They need to have their gifts and abilities stretched and used to the full in the service of Christ. Christian service must involve something bigger than keeping the life of the church ticking over. The much wider canvas of the Kingdom of God must be painted.

There is always the danger of the local church's monopolising the available time the men have to offer. Churches need to be prepared to release some of their men from committees and activities in order to be more deeply involved in areas of influence in the local community. Jesus said, 'You are the salt of the earth' and 'You are the light of the world' (Matt. 5:13, 14). But salt and light must be placed where they are needed most. Men of Christian conviction are needed on local councils, parent/teacher associations and other influential organisations which affect the quality of society. Churches often need to give greater support to their members who feel deeply about involvement in the life of the community.

In areas of unemployment the local church can take initiatives that will be a tangible demonstration that God cares. Men in the church can use their experience and gifts to help in a number of ways which may be appropriate in their community. Initiatives might include the following:

1. Start an unemployment group. Identify special needs of unemployed people in the locality.

2. Open a centre where people can meet for helpful counselling and advice.

3. Help adapt church premises for use as a drop-in or resource centre for action, information, leisure and recreation.

4. Join with others in setting up self-help groups.

5. Promote discussion in the congregation (home groups?) on the changing role of work in life.

6. Start a new business using existing local resources and skills.

In these and many other ways men, as well as women, can feel a far greater sense of fulfilment as agents of the Kingdom of God.

Men at Work

Too much preaching and teaching is unrelated to where men spend most of their working hours — in their jobs. 'How can I retain a Christian integrity in a fiercely competitive world where accepted values and standards are often in strong conflict?' 'What should my attitude as a Christian be to those I work with or those for whom I have a responsibility?' These and many other questions highlight the dilemma that many men face. Sunday services provide one of the main opportunities for spiritual inspiration and practical teaching.

If ministers are to anchor their teaching to the real, rather than the imagined, needs of men any opportunity should be taken to see where the men in their congregation work, and understand their pressures. For a minister to take a journey on a packed train at the beginning or end of a busy working day can be a salutary experience. It may well make him adjust his expectations of men in the church, who barely have time for a meal before coming out to this or that church activity.

The forum offered by informal home groups can likewise be a help in thrashing out issues that need a Christian perspective. Some churches also arrange regular prayer breakfasts for men so that problems can be shared and mutual encouragement given.

Keith Miller describes the painful process he went through when he first began to try and apply his Christian faith in the business world of which he was part. He managed to draw together a group of other men who had a similar concern:

> We found that it is not easy to take Christ into one's business as Lord. If one is serious, he soon realises that he must work harder than his non-Christian competitors and do a better job at his business, because he must give up the leverage of cutting corners (in the inevitable dishonest practices in business and taxation procedures). This may cost money ... a great deal of money.
>
> We came to realise that in the long run in our vocation the only real witness which would last was not what we said about our beliefs, but what people saw us to be week after week, in our dealings with our associates and our competitors.[22]

Reaching men for Christ is a major challenge confronting the Church today. It is a challenge which local church leaders dare not avoid.

Chapter 10

LISTENING TO OTHERS

It was Easter and one evening I was chatting to a guest who had come to Lee Abbey with his family. He began to ask a number of searching questions about the relevance of the Christian faith for his own life and handed me a poem he had written earlier in the day. He called it 'Drowning not Waving'.

> The sun shines so brightly
> The sky so blue.
> You think we are waving
> As happy as you.
> But has it occurred to you
> That we're apart –
> And we're drowning not waving –
> A cry from the heart.

'Everyone should be quick to listen, slow to speak and slow to become angry' (Jas. 1:19). The leader needs to be a listener. Too often those who lead don't listen. Clergy can be the main culprits. We preach and teach, lead discussion groups and chair meetings. Even when we are giving counsel to those seeking help we fall into the trap of being concerned only about what we can say. Christian leadership demands that we listen to others.

Jesus the Listener

St. John records a number of the encounters that Jesus had with individuals who crossed his path. Significantly, Jesus always listened to what was happening behind the words that the person was using. He was listening to the hidden and real needs rather than to their surface questions and attitudes. Nicodemus, a member of the Jewish ruling council, found his opening question bypassed when Jesus told him bluntly, 'I tell you the truth, unless a man is born again, he cannot see the Kingdom of God' (3:3). The listening Christ had discerned that this highly sophisticated religious leader was searching for a spiritual reality that so far had eluded him.

Jesus's encounter with the woman at the well at Sychar (Chapter 4) similarly shows him listening to what the woman is not saying rather than to what she is. Behind her conversational camouflage Jesus detects a deep yearning for acceptance, dignity and a quality of life that will satisfy her greatest longings.

Those who lead have to learn to listen with both ears. One ear concentrating on what the other person is saying and the other ear listening to what is not being said. A growing sensitivity to the Holy Spirit and a growing awareness of when and when not to speak make it possible to listen with both ears. Many people are 'drowning not waving' and need help.

Listening Involves Empathy

Empathy goes far deeper than sympathy. Sympathy involves feeling sorry for someone and attempting to say some carefully chosen words. But sympathy rarely penetrates the surface. Empathy is the attempt to enter right into another person's situation. There is nothing superficial or trite about empathy. The imagination has to be used and the heart moved. The Red Indian expression is 'walking in their moccasins'.

Jesus had an extraordinary capacity for empathy. On a number of occasions we read of his compassion for others in great need. The compassion that he felt for the leper, the widow of Nain, the spiritually and physically hungry, was something that he not only felt deeply but also responded to with love and majestic power.

Those who lead youth groups need to empathise with the frustrations and fears as well as the hopes and aspirations of the young. Those whose ministry takes them into regular contact with the elderly require a sensitivity to their inevitable uncertainties, caused by waning powers, as well as an appreciation of their accumulation of wisdom and experience.

Empathy for those who come alongside fractured marriages and families means absorbing some of the conflicting emotions, feeling the pain of rejection and helping to rebuild shattered lives. Those who jump in with words will often have nothing to say that makes any sense, but the one who listens first can become a channel of hope.

In caring for the bereaved the Christian minister or counsellor often has to listen and listen before any words are appropriate. The numbing sense of loss, the hopelessness and feeling of futility, the anger and the 'whys?' all have to be talked out. When Jesus heard of the death of his friend Lazarus he wept. Sometimes the most cathartic offering a listener can make is to share the grief of the broken-hearted.

Richard Gillard in 'The Servant Song' beautifully describes the empathy of the listener:

> I will hold the Christ-light for you
>   In the night-time of your fear;
> I will hold my hand out to you,
>   Speak the peace you long to hear.
>
> I will weep when you are weeping;
>   When you laugh I'll laugh with you.
> I will share your joy and sorrow
>   'Til we've seen this journey through.[23]

Listening Involves Enquiry

Christian leaders are often guilty of giving answers to questions that are not being asked; scratching where people are not itching. It can be true in the attitude and response to those who are regular church members. What is preached, taught and provided bears little relevance to people's real situations and needs. Assumptions are made and glib, though well-meaning, solutions offered that are a hindrance rather than a help towards spiritual growth. Listening involves enquiry.

For example, it is often assumed that the needs of a congregation or a group are the same as they were five years ago, whereas the whole dynamic will have changed. Some people will have moved and newcomers will have joined. There will be different levels of Christian experience as well as age. Some will only be on the nursery slopes of Christian awareness. Others will have travelled some distance in Christian discipleship. In addition, wider global and national issues will be different, and these changes must be taken into account. It is only when we listen with the spirit of enquiry and understanding that the good news of the Kingdom can be shared with relevance and confidence.

Listening must also involve an attitude of enquiry, otherwise we can become judgmental towards others. Instead of listening carefully and piecing together the salient facts that enable us to help with sensitivity and objectivity, our minds are already made up, and we have probably jumped to the wrong conclusion.

The judgmental approach of his so-called comforters drove Job to distraction. 'How long will you torment me and crush me with words? Ten times now you have reproached me; shamelessly you attack me' (Job 19:2–3). Their pat answers to the cause of his suffering revealed starkly their total inability to listen to Job with any real degree of empathy and enquiry. Proverbs provides a clear distinction between the bad and the good listener in chapter 18. 'He who answers before listening – that is his folly and his shame' (v. 13). Whereas, 'The heart of the discerning acquires knowledge; the ears of the wise seek it out' (v. 15).

That great missionary-statesman, Max Warren, wrote:

Listening to another person is a great deal more of an art than most of us realise. The true listener is giving all his attention to what the other person is saying, listening to even his silences.

Listening to Others

A subtler point still is, that as I so listen, I become aware of myself listening. This is important for, unless I listen to myself listening I will be likely to assume, quite wrongly, that a word used in the context of my own experience means the same as in the experience of the one to whom I am listening. There is much wisdom as well as a proper courtesy in this sensitivity of listening.

The Christian leader who is unprepared to give time to listen betrays a lack of Christ-like care and gentleness. 'Brothers, if someone is caught in a sin, you who are spiritual should restore him gently. But watch yourself, or you also may be tempted. Carry each other's burdens, and in this way you will fulfil the law of Christ' (Gal. 6:1–2). Christian leadership must involve sharing and carrying the burdens of others for whom there is any responsibility. The person bowed down by a burden, whether it is caused by sin or suffering, needs to be gently restored. To restore means to put something back in its rightful place, as with a broken limb so that it can be healed properly from within. If a leader is gentle, he is acting out a respect for the sensitivities of the other person and the seriousness of the problem. If he acts harshly or abruptly, then like the broken limb, the force applied can shatter rather than restore.

Listening in Evangelism

'Evangelism', as defined by D. T. Niles 'is like one beggar telling another beggar where to find bread.' I am assuming that everyone who has any part to play in the leadership in the local church will want to share Jesus, the Bread of Life, with others who are strangers to his love. Any church or Christian group that lives solely for itself stands guilty before God. Wilson Carlile, the founder of the Church Army, once said, 'I have got the biggest job I ever tackled in my life. I'm trying to open the mouths of people in the pews.' One of the greatest needs, if not the greatest, in the Church today is for ordinary Christians to be willing to share their faith, not in an attitude of superiority but like 'one beggar telling another beggar where to find bread.'

The good news of Christ is for us to pass on to others with sensitivity, integrity and boldness. But to do this effectively, listening must figure prominently in our evangelism. People came to realise and expose their real needs to Jesus because they knew they could depend on his listening to them. After he had listened he then spoke the word of life that transformed their own lives and situations. Only as we take time to listen to the longings and fears, the questions and difficulties of others can we begin to have any understanding of how to interpret the good news for them. There can be no effective evangelism without listening.

Raymond Fung, in his monthly letter on evangelism (March 1982) describes how during the first five years of his involvement among the poor in Hong Kong, he and his colleagues were not able, and did not dare, to engage in evangelism among working-class people. At that time the Christian Church had no base among the working-class and no credibility. He writes,

> Our university and middle class background, for which no apology was required, did not qualify us to be evangelists among the poor. It had only made us aware of the need to listen. So we did. We listened to the men and women working in the textile mills and electronic plants. Then we were able to speak to them about each other, about friends and families, about visiting those injured at work, about the city's injustice, the need to organise for power, and about Jesus. And what message have we found for the factory workers in Hong Kong? What is God's word to them in their situation? What have we been speaking to them as we listen to them? Essentially, in our case, it is the word of Jesus: 'Take up your cross and follow me. I have heard you. I know you. I am with you. But I have a task, a tough and costly task. Come, join me. Let us go together.'

In this way Raymond Fung and his co-workers shared the Bread of Life with people in their weakness and in their strength.

Substitute your own town or village for Hong Kong. Look

at the social and cultural setting in which your church, the local expression of the Body of Christ, is set. Look at your family, friends and neighbours and at where you work for much of your waking life. In the rightful concern to make Jesus better known, how much care and time is being given to listening?

In the monasteries of the Russian Orthodox Church during the last couple of centuries, certain men were recognised as having an extraordinary degree of spiritual discernment. They were not appointed to any special position, but a large number of men and women, both rich and poor, came from all over Russia to consult the Startsy, as they were called. Many were healed of both spiritual and bodily ills, and many more received advice which changed their lives. The greatest of the Startsy seem to have known the names and troubles of people who came to see them before they were told.

What was the secret of the Startsy? It was found in the closeness of their relationship with God in a life of disciplined prayer and contemplation. It was seen in lives imbued with the Holy Spirit. They were men who listened to the Spirit as they listened to those who sought their counsel and help. They were channels of that same Spirit bringing healing and hope, wisdom and strength.

The Christian leader can also be a channel of the Holy Spirit as he listens to others. The Holy Spirit is the 'paraclete', the one who is called on for assistance. He is the Comforter and Counsellor. When time is given to listen to God and to others, the Holy Spirit comes to the aid of our weakness and gives us his discernment and words.

Chapter 11

SHARING THE VISION

Lee Abbey Community members take it in turn to lead morning
worship. An American startled and amused us one day by
declaring, 'If you can't see beyond a hamburger you will never
eat steak!' It was an unusual but highly memorable way of
emphasising the need to beware of complacency and of
challenging us to enlarge our vision.

Every Christian leader needs to have vision. Whether it be
the leadership of a congregation or a prayer group, a choir
or a youth club, vision is imperative. We must have a vision
for the work that God has entrusted to us. Vision is all about
seeing beyond what has already been accomplished to what
God has in mind for the future. Leadership without vision is
doomed to mediocrity and even failure. Sadly, many Christian
leaders haven't any vision or desire for it. They may have had
vision in the past but now they are content to rest on the laurels
of past achievements. The sense of expectancy that God may
be wanting to do 'a new thing' is no longer present. Charles
Sorenson once said: 'It isn't the incompetents who destroy an
organisation. The incompetent never gets in a position to
destroy it – it is those who have achieved something and want
to rest upon their achievements who are forever clogging things
up.' Though his remarks have industry in mind, they could
equally well be applied to visionless leadership in the local
church.

Nehemiah

Nehemiah was a man of vision. He came to the fore at a point when national life had reached rock bottom. Israel had been overrun by the Babylonian armies. Jerusalem had been plundered. Her buildings — including the Temple, had been destroyed and the city walls razed to the ground. Many of her leading citizens, including Nehemiah, had been carried off into exile. Those left behind were dispirited and listless. Above all, they were leaderless. They saw no hope for the future and even believed that God had deserted them. Vision was a thing of the past.

The return of Nehemiah to Jerusalem completely changed the picture. The way he tackled the colossal task that confronted him is a superb example of visionary leadership. The Book of Nehemiah should be required reading for anyone involved in Christian leadership!

Realistic Assessment

Nehemiah's first task was to make a careful reconnoitre of the city boundaries, examining the broken-down walls and the charred gates. By doing this Nehemiah was under no illusion of the immensity of the challenge that lay ahead. His vision of a rebuilt city and a renewed people was not some kind of fantasy trip that was totally unrelated to the realities of the situation. He knew the facts and the vision God gave him took these facts fully into consideration.

There was no escaping the facts when Dick Sheppard became Vicar of St. Martin-in-the-Fields in the heart of London: only eleven people came to the Institution Service on a foggy November morning in 1918, but with those eleven he shared his vision for the future ministry at St. Martin's. It was a vision that he believed God had given him in the trenches during the war years, of a church where many hundreds of people would find acceptance and hope. He had a passionate concern that all who entered the doors of St. Martin's should learn of the love of Jesus Christ and should then go out into the streets of London to share that love with others.

> Will you give a hand in trying, even if we fail, to build up this church, in the greatest city in the world? ... There may be someone of you who has little to offer. One who is thinking to himself or herself, 'It's a great scheme, can it be done? Have I anything to offer?' To you, most of all, I would say that you have wonderful things to offer.[25]

From such small, unpromising beginnings a new work at St. Martin's was launched. It was to become famous throughout the world.

Realistic assessment is important in any sphere of Christian work, whether it be large or small. The resources available, the problems to be faced, and the available support are all facts to be taken into account. Against this background a vision then needs to be grasped of what can happen in the future. Jesus knew the facts when a large crowd needed to be fed. They numbered over five thousand and the resources to meet their hunger were tiny. Five small barley loaves and two fish – only enough for a young boy's picnic lunch – but Jesus could see what could be done with such an offering and in his hands the bread and fish became food for all. James S. Stewart said, 'We have allowed the magnitude of our problems to blind us to the majesty of our Master.' A vision of the greatness of Christ helps us to see our problems in perspective and to overcome them.

Prayerful Reflection

Vision is born out of prayer. Nehemiah was a man of prayer. When his brother had first brought him news of the abysmal state of affairs in Jerusalem, Nehemiah's first reaction had been to weep, fast and pray. He felt deeply the pain of his people, identifying himself with the disobedience and rebellion against

God that had brought suffering upon their heads. But as he prayed he was not slow to remind God of his promise that 'If you return to me and obey my commands, then even if your exiled people are at the farthest horizon, I will gather them from there and bring them to the place I have chosen as a dwelling for my name.' (1 v. 9). This insight into Nehemiah at prayer reveals the secret of what then was to follow. Re-kindled hope and the vision of a resurrected Jerusalem began to emerge as he offered himself as a leader whom God could use.

Prayerful reflection is essential for there to be vision. Suffici-ent time has to be given to allow God to pass on his thoughts, plans and directions to those he entrusts with the responsibility of leadership. Every leader needs a 'bolthole' to which he can retreat in order to advance. St. Julian's in Coolham, Sussex, is such a place. The beautiful grounds which include a lake, the quiet and orderliness of the house with its well-stocked library and simple chapel and, above all, the unobtrusive, caring service of the Community, make St. Julian's an oasis of refreshment and re-creative thinking for its guests. On a number of occasions it has been the place where my own priorities have been reshaped, my spirit has been quickened and there has come the mounting excitement of renewed vision for my ministry.

To get away to a St. Julian's will not always be possible or practical. Yet the need remains for those who lead to find space to wait upon God in order to receive fresh vision from him. Every local church will have somewhere near at hand to which leaders can go and spend time together in prayer and discussion. Members of my former congregation who lived out-side the parish gladly offered the hospitality of their homes so that our church leaders could periodically spend a day of reflection. These occasions would often prove to be significant points of fresh vision and direction as we set our sails to catch the wind of the Spirit.

High up in the Cotswold hills lies the small town of North-leach, which is the centre of a deanery of a number of scattered villages. Over the last fifteen years many facilities and services have been lost: village shops, post offices, schools and buses In spite of cutbacks in the number of clergy, congregations in the area have risen to the challenge and members have become more deeply involved in the life of the local community as well as the church.

At the heart of the Northleach Deanery is a small committee led by Canon Arthur Dodds, the Rural Dean. Over the years though the personnel may have changed, this committee has become a group of people who are completely open with each other and pray naturally together as they seek how to further God's Kingdom of love in the area. Prayer is behind every endeavour and is the springboard of fresh vision. There is a vibrant sense of purpose about the worship, fellowship and witness of the churches.

The hallmark of vision is that it has a forward thrust. It challenges entrenched positions and attitudes that cling to the past and stubbornly resist change. The Kingdom of God is always best served by going forward, never by going back and staying in the wilderness, making our tent pegs more secure. Paul Tournier said, 'It is by going forward from one adventure to another that a movement stays alive. Saying "Yes" to God is saying "Yes" to life ... to life with all its problems and difficulties. "Yes" instead of "No" is an attitude of adventure instead of going on strike.'[26] The people of God are a pilgrim people: 'Here we have no lasting city, but we seek the city which is to come' (Heb. 13:14, RSV). The fresh vision that takes a church forward, out of the ruts of apathy and complacency, is conceived during the times apart with God in prayer.

Infectious Enthusiasm

To be enthused means to be 'full of God'. Each of us is as full of God as we really want to be. Leaders are needed in the local church who are enthused with God and in turn are able to share their vision and persuade others to play their part in its realisation.

Nehemiah shared his vision with infectious enthusiasm. He

gathered together the priests, nobles and officials and told them, ' "You see the trouble we are in: Jerusalem lies in ruins, and its gates have been burned with fire. Come, let us rebuild the walls of Jerusalem, and we will no longer be in disgrace." I also told them about the gracious hand of my God upon me' (2:17, 18).

The response was immediate, ' "Let us start rebuilding." So they began this good work' (v. 18). In the weeks that followed priests and people worked side by side to rebuild the city walls. Everyone had a part to play. Each knew that his contribution was important. Morale began to soar as the seemingly impossible was seen to be possible. In the forefront of all the activity Nehemiah moved among the workers encouraging and enthusing them to complete the job.

It was a maxim of Field-Marshal Montgomery that 'Every single soldier must know, before he goes into battle, how the little battle he is to fight fits into the larger picture, and how the success of his fighting will influence the battle as a whole.'[27] In the same way that Dick Sheppard had the capacity to share his vision for the developing ministry of St. Martin-in-the-Fields so that everyone could feel involved, leaders in the local church need to be able to persuade others to help them translate vision into reality. The most effective form of persuasion is infectious enthusiasm.

'The Last Great Journey in the World' was how the press in 1953 described the plan of Dr. Vivian Fuchs to make the first crossing of the Antarctic continent over the South Pole. Edmund Hillary, conquerer of Everest, was invited to lead the New Zealand party involved in the expedition. In his auto-biography, *Nothing Venture, Nothing Win*, he describes his first meeting with Dr. Fuchs.

Fuchs was a square, strongly built man with a formidable air of determination and toughness. His manner was quite abrupt and even awkward until he started talking about his plans and then the words flowed with eager enthusiasm. He detailed his intentions, using the stem of his pipe to point out the route on a large map of the Antarctic, and became completely immersed in the story although he must have told it a hundred times before.[28]

Edmund Hillary caught the vision that Vivian Fuchs shared with such infectious enthusiasm, and he became an important part of its fulfilment. He and his polar expedition were winners of the Antarctic race and the first men to trek to the Pole in forty-six years.

Infectious enthusiasm is a quality that every leader needs if he is going to persuade others to share his vision fully. He must be humble enough to allow others to test his vision, but once this has been done he must do all in his power to make it become a corporate vision. God never means vision to be confined to those in key positions of leadership. Vision has to be conveyed and shared so that others can catch the excitement of its significance and see it come to fruition.

Unstoppable Determination

Infectious enthusiasm needs to be accompanied by unstoppable determination. Enthusiasm without determination can evaporate into thin air. Determination anchors enthusiasm and ensures that the vision is not lost until it has been accomplished.

Nehemiah's determination is a striking feature of his leadership. Humanly speaking the odds against success were enormous. But Nehemiah was single-minded in his determination to see the job finished. He refused to be diverted by internal grievances and by external pressures from those who stood to lose once the walls of Jerusalem had been rebuilt. Jerusalem's enemies – Sanballat, Tobiah and others – tried every threat and ruse they knew in order to intimidate Nehemiah and halt the building operations. But Nehemiah was constantly on his guard and was quick to anticipate and counter their machinations. Work continued until the walls stood proudly erect. With the utmost simplicity the climax is recorded, 'So the wall was completed on the twenty-fifth of Elul, in fifty-two days' (6:15). Another entry for the Guinness Book of Records!

Nehemiah's vision for Jerusalem didn't end with the re-building of the walls. It was a crucial project to complete if the inhabitants of the city were to feel secure and regain their sense of identity. But far more important, Nehemiah believed that the project would be a means of knitting the people together in renewed confidence and trust in the living God who alone could give them a future and a hope. Great was his joy in seeing this larger vision fulfilled.

Why give examples of men like Nehemiah whose vision and consequent achievements have become legendary? Not to depress, but rather to encourage us to dream dreams and to have visions that reflect the greatness of the God we serve. Too often our horizons are limited and our thinking far too small.

If God has assigned us a task of leadership and responsibility he will not want us to forget that however small the beginnings the possibilities are limitless. After all, he is the God of the galaxies!

Chapter 12

DELEGATING RESPONSIBILITY

Shortly after moving to a new parish the vicar wrote to me:
'So far it's been a case of getting on with the routine of daily
parish life. All that is done within the parish is expected to
be done by the priest and his wife — regardless of the fact that
mine has a full-time occupation as a sister in the local hospital!
That had been the pattern previously and so there were no
doubt sighs of relief when I arrived, that everything could be
dumped on my lap, as it literally was! Keys by the dozen — some
of which I haven't a clue where they belong — papers, old
folders, some of which should have been thrown away long
ago.'

This minister had a sizeable challenge to face. His case is
not an isolated one. In spite of the fact that shared responsibility is now being taken more seriously in many churches, there
are still many congregations where leadership is seen to reside
in one person only. Sometimes the fault lies with the minister.
What he says goes and woe betide anyone who challenges his
authority. In other churches it is the congregation who call
the tune. They expect their minister to do everything of
practical as well as pastoral significance. 'That's what he's paid
for', they argue. But it is an argument that is full of holes and
a sure recipe for spiritual stagnation and total ineffectiveness
in the local community. Shared responsibility and delegation
are essential.

Delegating Responsibility

Wise Father-in-Law

When Jethro went to visit his son-in-law he saw immediately that Moses was carrying too much responsibility on his own shoulders. Jethro took him to task: 'What is this you are doing to the people? Why do you alone sit and judge, while all these people stand around you from morning to evening? What you are doing is not good. You and these people who come to you will only wear yourselves out. The work is too heavy for you; you cannot handle it alone' (Exod. 18:14, 17, 18). Jethro then proposed that Moses should continue to act as God's representative, responsible for the teaching of spiritual principles and exercising his legislative functions, but he should delegate other areas of judicial responsibility to competent men. By doing this Moses could concentrate on the more important aspects of his leadership, at the same time making it possible for others to share responsibility and be trained in the art of leadership.

The qualities of leadership that Jethro suggested reveal his spiritual discernment. 'Select capable men from all the people — men who fear God, trustworthy men who hate dishonest gain — and appoint them as officials over thousands, hundreds, fifties and tens' (v. 21). Moses was humble enough to listen to his father-in-law and accept his advice. He chose seventy leaders and delegated responsibility to them for assisting in the care of the people of Israel.

Oversight in the Early Church

Whenever Paul founded churches in his missionary travels, he would make a point of returning at the earliest opportunity to select and appoint elders. For example, when Paul and Barnabas returned to Lystra, Iconium and Antioch, they 'appointed elders for them in each church and, with prayer and fasting, committed them to the Lord in whom they had put their trust' (Acts 14:23).

The responsibilities entrusted to elders were varied. They were to be 'shepherds of God's flock that is under your care' (1 Pet. 5:2). They were to heal the sick (Jas. 5:14). Some were to engage in preaching and teaching (1 Tim. 5:17). Evangelism was also to be part of their concern (Acts 20:28). Paul reminds the Ephesian elders of how 'I have declared to both Jews and Greeks that they must turn to God in repentance and have faith in our Lord Jesus' (v. 21). The apostle clearly expected them to follow his example.

The five-fold gifts for ministry — apostles, prophets, evangelists, pastors and teachers (Eph. 4:11) — would not have been confined to the eldership of the local church. Some of these gifts would have been evident among other members. Nevertheless the elders would have exercised different gifts and ministries in order to provide the range of oversight necessary 'to prepare God's people for works of service, so that the body of Christ may be built up' (v. 12). With shared responsibilities of this kind it is not surprising that the New Testament declares that the authority of elders is to be recognised and they are to be held in the highest regard in love because of their work (1 Thess. 5:12, 13).

Putting it into Practice

For both biblical and practical reasons many churches whose traditions and practice had previously excluded the concept of 'elders' are now introducing them. Certainly the term 'elder' has won wider acceptance. In addition to its strong link with the New Testament, the word indicates someone of spiritual maturity and wisdom as well as someone respected for other qualities both in the church and in the local community. Invariably the introduction of an eldership scheme has proved a significant step forward in the life of the church.

Various methods are used in the choice and appointment of elders. Some churches choose them, after prior discussion and prayer, at a specially convened meeting of members. In other cases, the minister proposes names for consideration and approval by the church council. It is important that the minister himself feels secure in this process. For this reason an eldership scheme stands the best chance of getting off the ground if the initiative has come from the minister (even if he has been prodded into action by concerned members of the congregation!) If he is wise the minister will carefully consult his church officers and will do all he can to ensure that those chosen have the full backing of the church membership.

David Watson describes what happened when he became convinced that 'pastoral elders' should be introduced at St. Cuthbert's, York:

> I asked the congregation to pray about the matter for a week, and then to submit to me in writing the names of up to seven men. These men had to be recognised as being 'full of faith and of the Holy Spirit', and it should be obvious to all that God was already using them in pastoral counselling. Naturally I prayed much as well, and by the end of the week chose six men who seemed to me to be most fitted for this work. It was clear confirmation for me when the nominations sent in by the congregation tallied exactly with those on my own list![29]

When I was Vicar of St. Andrew's, Chorleywood, I felt at one stage, as did others, that it was time to strengthen the pastoral care of the congregation. I was fortunate to have a team of full-time members of staff working with me but numbers had grown considerably and we were conscious that pastoral care was becoming increasingly superficial. I believe that the appointment of a pastoral group at that stage helped to bring a greater strength, cohesion and direction to the whole life of the church. We met once a week to pray and discuss matters of pastoral concern. It also provided an ideal forum in which to test ideas and assess the spiritual temperature of the church and work out appropriate teaching and training programmes. I found this group a constant source of strength and support as we shared together in an atmosphere of mutual trust.

Pastoral elders can also have a very important role to play in rural or inner-city churches where numbers may be much smaller, and where often the minister has to care for more than one congregation. The appointment of a few carefully chosen men and women to share in the pastoral oversight helps to strengthen the fellowship and witness of the congregation(s).

Furthermore, it is in rural and inner-city areas that many ministers feel most isolated. The prayer and practical support and wisdom of a small group of elders can revolutionise their ministries. They can become 'possibility-thinkers' instead of trying desperately to cope alone with a seemingly impossible load of responsibility on their shoulders.

The sharing of pastoral responsibility with a group of elders provides a necessary check on a minister. If, previously, he had seen himself as 'six feet above contradiction', he dare not do so any longer! The other elders will not let him get away with it. He is expressing his need of them, just as they need him. In turn, by sharing his ministry in this way, he is enabling his fellow elders to appreciate the particular pressures and demands, as well as the many rewards, that come with leadership in the local church. It will also be one sure way of making the minister more aware of what they have to face in their own lives. Ministers are not always good at being sensitive to the pressures that many Christians have to cope with.

Check-points

When shared leadership is being introduced into a church, great care needs to be taken to ensure that its purpose is as widely understood as possible. The 'we have always done it this way' brigade will resist change and their views must be weighed up and not ignored. The steamroller approach is the quickest way to create disharmony and division. A series of sermons may well be necessary to help prepare the way so that the biblical principles and their practical application can be carefully explained. Articles in the church magazine or newsletter may need to be written. A question and answer session at a meeting of the congregation may be appropriate. Individual church members may need to be visited and their uncertainties or objections listened to carefully. When all this has been done, and the conviction is even stronger that the time is right to go ahead, then the step should be taken. Hopefully it will not be long before the congregation feels an even greater sense of being cared for by its spiritual leaders.

It is important that the introduction and functioning of a pastoral eldership group should not interfere with the role of other church committees. The lines of demarcation in responsibility should be clearly drawn, understood and respected. For example, elders will not normally decide church policy and priorities. The Church Council will be the appropriate body to deal with these matters, though the elders may from time to time bring forward suggestions and recommendations for discussion and decision. An eldership group can be a kind of 'vision-tank' but the objective assessment of the Church Council as a 'check-tank' is often needed.

It is generally wise for elders to be appointed for a specific period of time rather than it be assumed that they are there for life. Some churches adopt a fixed three-year period of office with the possibility of recommissioning for a further period. My own view is that three years is generally too short, but it underlines the important principle of having a regular re-evaluation of the congregation's spiritual oversight. It also allows other mature Christians the opportunity to take their turn as pastoral elders. Furthermore, the 'retiring' elders are able to use their wisdom and experience to strengthen other areas in the life of the church.

In the delegation of responsibility risks have to be taken if God's purpose for a local church is going to be fulfilled. The perceptive leader will generally be able to sense what other people are capable of achieving. He will want to do all in his power to help them make the most of their new opportunities, making it clear what he expects from them and be there to support when any uncertainties arise. It can be discouraging to be delegated a responsibility without help and guidance as to how it can best be done. A sensitive awareness of both the problems and the opportunities is important on the part of the delegator. Constant encouragement and appreciation always brings out the best in others, not least from those who share pastoral responsibilities.

John Garnett, Director of the Industrial Society, makes the helpful point that people engaged in a common task need to know four things:

a) What am I being asked to do?

b) Who am I accountable to?

c) How am I getting on?

d) Where do I go for help?

These same questions are a healthy check to any scheme for delegating or sharing responsibility in the church. The minister, in particular, needs to be able to answer them clearly.

One thing is certain. The wise sharing of responsibility ensures that a steady stream of leaders is being trained and used in the local church. The minister who is prepared to share responsibility with others is not only helping to provide a stronger core of leadership where it is needed most, but is also ensuring that he is not making himself indispensable when the time comes to move to another sphere of work.

A senior trade unionist once commented: 'What we want now are leaders not bosses.' If this is true in industry, commerce and the public services it is also true in the local church. An effective Christian leader is essentially one who is willing to delegate responsibility to others and is able to work happily with them.

Chapter 13

LEADING IN THE HOME

One of the most exciting features of the past twenty years has been the re-emergence of the home as a meeting place for Christians. Variously described as home groups, cells, or support fellowships they have become an essential and integral part of the life and strategy of many local churches. In the informality, group members have found the help they have needed for spiritual growth coupled with a deeper quality of fellowship. Furthermore, many home groups have become a springboard for effective evangelism and social action in their neighbourhoods.

There is, of course, nothing new about all this. From the earliest days of the Church Christians met in homes. 'They broke bread in their homes and ate together with glad and sincere hearts, praising God and enjoying the favour of all the people' (Acts 2:46, 47). Within a few weeks of the Day of Pentecost there were at least 12,000 Christians meeting all over Jerusalem in private homes. I like to think that the 120 who were filled with the Spirit at Pentecost were the first home group leaders!

The home was the natural place for the first Christians to meet. It was the focal point of Jewish life. They continued to worship in the temple, but the home was the principal place where 'they devoted themselves to the Apostles' teaching and to the fellowship, to the breaking of bread and to prayer' (v. 42). Later in Acts we find the first Philippian converts meeting in the home of Lydia (16:40) and in Ephesus Paul declares how he taught publicly and from house to house (20:20).

During his remarkable ministry in the eighteenth century,

John Wesley established class-meetings or 'nurture cells', as Wesleyans have called them. These nurture cells for new Christians were an essential part of his strategy. Wesley's ideal number for each cell was about eight to twelve. It is perhaps significant that Jesus concentrated a lot of his teaching and training on a group of twelve.

In South America there was a phenomenal growth of the Church in the 1950s and 1960s. The two principal reasons were as follows:

First, the emphasis on the infilling and the work of the Holy Spirit. Second, the fact that in South America they adopt a cell structure – many thousands of small groups meeting in private homes in countries such as Brazil and Bolivia. These cells are appropriately called 'nuclear cells'.

My first experience of a regular pattern of home groups was when Canon Harry Sutton came to Chorleywood to lead a parish mission. A number of home meetings were organised as part of the programme. Following the mission there was a strong plea that some of the home meetings should continue on a more regular basis and they became the nucleus of a growing structure of groups throughout the parish. In the years that followed about 300 people became regular members of evening home groups. The groups met every other Wednesday, alternating with a Church Family Night when all came together for corporate worship, teaching and prayer.

Being Yourself

Many church members are unsure of what they believe. They want to know but there is little opportunity to 'come back' at the preacher on Sunday, so most people cope by creating a false ring of confidence in order to cover their ignorance. This is where the home group scores. In the relaxed and informal atmosphere of the home, members can be themselves. Doubts as well as convictions can be voiced. Heresies – and all of us have some of them – can be freely expressed without others' being shocked. Consequently, for many people a home group has been the setting in which their faith in Jesus Christ has come alive or matured.

It means, of course, that the group leader's approach has to be non-judgmental. At the same time the leader needs to be able to answer questions as adequately as possible. For this to happen the leader will have to prepare for the evening as thoroughly as possible in order to be at least one step ahead of the rest of the group.

Sensitivity to the different people present will always be important. Patience will be required with any who are slow to formulate their ideas. Firmness and courtesy will be necessary when one or more members try to dominate the group. Some leaders are 'naturals' but most have to learn as they go along. It is no easy task but infinitely worthwhile to see a group increasingly fulfil its potential.

Building Foundations

After Pentecost, the Apostles' teaching was spread and discussed in homes throughout Jerusalem. Foundations for Christian belief and living were built and strengthened.

The home group offers untold opportunities for the full use of the teaching and learning process. It generally needs to have a definite scheme of study for discussion so that knowledge can be imparted as well as experience shared. Moreover, a definite course of study helps to prevent a group from becoming too subjective. There is no lack of group study material available – outlines from biblical books and themes, doctrinal subjects, moral and ethical questions, obstacles to faith, topical global themes and so on. Tape 'discussion starters' can be very effective and the advent of video offers exciting new possibilities for teaching and discussion in the home.

Some churches produce their own material for home groups and this can have the advantage of being more directly tailor-made for the particular needs of the group. At one stage I produced a series of simple outlines on 'God's Church Today' and over the course of several months all the parish home groups studied and discussed its various themes. At Lee Abbey we find we have considerable demand for home group resource material and have produced a fairly wide range of printed and tape study outlines.

In helping to build foundations, the home group leader will want to use study material that is relevant to the composition of the group and the point it has reached. It will be little use tackling a series of studies which presuppose a basic understanding of the Christian faith when the group is largely composed of enquirers or new Christians. In the same way, a group which is well past the beginners stage will want to use a course of studies that will stretch their minds rather than take them back over familiar ground. For this reason, though there will be occasions when it is right for all home groups linked to a local church to study the same material (e.g. in preparation for a mission), generally it is important for each group to find its own level. The leader, therefore, has to be alert to the needs of the group, take careful soundings with the members and find appropriate teaching material.

The regular use of questions is important in the teaching and learning process. A good home group leader will want to use questions to stimulate discussion and tease out answers that will make everyone think. Jesus often used the question/ answer method with his disciples. 'Who do the crowds say I am?' was a very good question to start them talking. Back came a number of answers. Then Jesus was able to take them a stage farther to ask the next significant question quite naturally, 'but what about you? who do you say I am?' In reply, Peter made his great confession of faith, 'The Christ of God' (Luke 9:18, 20).

Caring for One Another

Fellowship has sometimes been caricatured as cheerful back-slapping. In contrast, the New Testament Greek word for fellowship (*koinonia*), is derived from *koinonos*, which is translated partner, companion, partaker, sharer. True biblical fellowship is a full, open, warm sharing of one's life and spirit with others.

The greatest need of our time is for *koinonia*, the call simply to be the church, to love one another, and to offer our lives for the sake of the world. The creation of living, breathing, loving communities of faith at the local church level is the foundation of all the other answers. The community of faith incarnates a whole new order, offers a visible and concrete alternative, and issues a basic challenge to the world as it is.[30]

It is in the home group that the true meaning of fellowship, as a partnership of giving and receiving, can be more deeply explored and enjoyed. The group can learn to develop a corporate sense of identity — a sense of belonging and caring for one another, and a growing openness to each other and to the Holy Spirit.

The home group, like the local church of which it is part, is a gathering of people who would not necessarily choose one another as friends. This is perhaps one of its greatest strengths. From the rubbing together of dissimilar personalities some of the greatest discoveries can emerge. And bridges can be built that help individuals and enhance their relationships. It is in a caring atmosphere of a home group that the free flow of Christian love can be experienced as members learn to accept one another, support one another and share one another's joys and sorrows.

Growth in the depth of fellowship in a group does not take place overnight. An attitude of wary superficiality can persist for some time. The breakthrough may come when one of the members shares a deep need and asks for the prayers and advice of the group. Perceptively the dynamics of the group begin to change. The open sharing of a need in this way can also act as a trigger to bring others' needs to the surface from within the group.

It is often the leader, however, who influences the quality of fellowship within the group. The leader has the power to keep relationships at a level of neutral politeness or he can help open them up in mutual trust and support. The most effective home group leader is the one who is prepared to be open about his own life and about his own need to be a receiving as well as a giving member of the group.

To further cement the fellowship of the group a simple, informal service of Holy Communion may be held in the room where they meet. Through Sacrament as well as through Word, Christ makes himself known to us and as the group feed by faith upon him members are not only expressing their joyful dependence on Christ but also their dependence on one another.

Looking Outward

The greatest danger for the home group is insularity. The temptation is always strong within any close-knit group of people to keep others at bay and be unconcerned about what is happening in the world. Where a home group becomes introspective and insular, it soon loses its true identity and purpose. In the end it shrivels and dies. The Dead Sea is dead because it has no outflow. Every home group should have an outflow into the wider life of the immediate neighbourhood and beyond. The early Church grew at such a rate because it was inclusive, not exclusive. 'The Lord added to their number daily those who were being saved' (Acts 2:47).

In the strategy of the local church home groups can be located in different parts of the area, thereby extending its pastoral, evangelistic and social concern. For this reason, it is often more effective if people belong to a home group in their own road or vicinity. The group then consists of those who have a genuine identification with the immediate area. They know it and are in touch with what is going on. In this way the group can become a channel of the love of Christ to those around. When Mrs W. is taken into hospital, the group has her in their hearts in prayer and does what it can to offer practical help. When a dispute arises between neighbours, members of the group may be able to act as arbiters and effect reconciliation. The opportunities for prayerful, supportive caring will be endless.

Where a home group is looking outward, there will be a natural overspill of the love of Jesus. It is this that makes the most powerful evangelistic effect on a locality. There will be occasions when it will be right for the home group to have special evenings when neighbours can be invited to hear a guest speak on a theme that presents thoughtfully and relevantly the claims of Christ. Two questions about the Christian gospel are often in the minds of many people who do not belong to a church: 'Is it true?' 'Does it work?' They are unprepared to come to a church service to try to find the answers, but a home is a different matter. In the relaxed atmosphere of a home they are much more likely to listen and question. Rightly, they will be looking for evidence in the lives of Christians that what they say they believe is making a difference. Some people are outside the church because those they know in it are half-hearted. On one occasion I was at a home meeting when a young woman, who had only been to church twice in her life, said, 'Christianity is either a big con trick, or you have to give it everything.' The home meeting can be a bridge for some to find Christ and then to become part of the family of his Church.

Barry Kissell was a colleague in Chorleywood. He has the gift of the evangelist, but has always strongly believed that the most powerful evangelistic tool is the corporate commitment of a group of Christians to Jesus Christ, to one another and to the world. Over the years he has worked to challenge and help the home groups scattered throughout the area to be more concerned for their neighbours and to find fresh ways of sharing their faith with them. Furthermore, he has trained, taken and sent teams to many parts of the country in order to bring encouragement and help where it is needed.

Barry believes that a home group makes a very effective evangelistic team and sometimes a whole home group will be one of the 'away' teams for a weekend helping in another parish. Barry once said, 'All together we are a reflection of the life of Christ. We enjoy fellowship and our sharing is an expression of what we are discovering together. Corporately, we can show the evidence of Christ in our lives. We can show the way to worship him, and the way we must live.' Again and again, it is in the relaxed and receptive setting of a home that the biggest impact of a team is made.

John tells us that 'The Word became flesh and lived for a while among us' (1:14). Incarnational evangelism is where the living Christ is seen, not just heard, through the lives, the attitudes and actions of those who have been set free by his love and want to share that love with others. The home group leader has the responsibility to keep reminding the group that the same love that binds them together is not to be hoarded or jealously guarded but freely distributed. The home group must keep its face turned to the world.

Supporting the Leaders

Those who lead home groups need careful back-up, encouragement and training. To appoint leaders is not the end of the matter! A caring, watchful eye must be kept on them. The minister, if he is wise, will beware of too much interference or of trying to dampen initiative. Where someone is asked to do a job they must be given the space to get on with it. At the same time, the special demands of home group leadership require frequent attention.

The minister will need to keep in touch with each leader on a one-to-one basis. Home groups require careful monitoring. Where a group gets too large it needs to be divided so that growth can continue. Where a group is sickly or turned-in on itself, it may need to close or be given an injection of new life by the introduction of one or two members from another, flourishing group.

Regular meetings of home group leaders are important. These provide the opportunity for feed-back. Leaders can share matters of mutual interest and concern. Ideas can be exchanged and difficulties discussed. Plans can be made for future development. Training can be given to help equip each leader in how to lead a discussion, how to encourage group members to contribute, how to identify particular gifts and needs, how to plan an evangelistic home meeting. Undergirded by meeting and praying together, leaders are better able to fulfil their responsibilities.

One final word. It is not the quantity but the quality of home groups that is all-important. Quality is related to leadership.

Chapter 14

BEWARE OF IDOLATRY

Idolatry is the worship of people or things in the place of God. That which commands our time, energy and thoughts is what we really worship. Leaders are specially prone to idolatry. Either they put themselves on a pedestal or allow others to do it for them. Many a congregation has suffered because its leader has fallen victim to the sin of idolatry and come crashing down. The pieces take a long time to put together. Many homes of Christian leaders have been shaken or wrecked because of idolatry. Let every Christian leader beware of idolatry.

> The dearest idol I have known
> Whate'er that idol be,
> Help me to tear it from Thy throne
> And worship only Thee.[31]

The Peril of Pride

The root cause of idolatry is pride. It was said of Hudson Taylor, founder of the Cina Inland Mission (now the Overseas Missionary Fellowship), 'He was a man small enough for God to use.' God is unable to use the leader who has become puffed up and proud through being in a position of responsibility. Pride of achievement, success and popularity, pride of 'my church', 'my theological position', 'my group or club', 'my ability to speak, teach or organise', 'my spiritual gifts', 'my way of doing things' are all danger areas for the Christian leader. Spiritual pride is particularly insidious. We can so easily create our own idols and justify them by giving them a 'God-stamp' of approval.

Spiritual arrogance was the cause of the downfall of King Saul. No leader could have begun with more promise and acclaim. Initially, he showed all the signs of a humble dependence on the God who had chosen and appointed him. But as time went on Saul allowed the status of his high office to blur his recognition that all power belongs to God. He took actions and made decisions that were not his to take or make and the account of his spiritual and mental deterioration and his rejection by God as the leader of his people makes tragic reading. It acts as a solemn warning of the peril of pride.

The prophets were often unpopular in their day because they ruthlessly exposed the idolatrous pride of the religious leaders. They castigated the outward show of religious practices and ceremonial. They condemned the lack of inner reality and of a genuine concern for justice and righteousness.

> I hate, I despise your
>   religious feasts;
> I cannot stand your
>   assemblies.
>
> let justice roll on like a
>   river,
> righteousness like a
>   never-failing stream!
>   (Amos 5:21, 24)

Jesus, likewise, ruthlessly exposed the pride and hypocrisy of many of the religious leaders he met. Their fastidious preoccupation with outward purification met his scathing denunciation. 'You Pharisees clean the outside of the cup and dish, but inside you are full of greed and wickedness' (Luke 11:39). Their self-importance came under his public condemnation. 'Woe to you Pharisees, because you love the most important seats in the synagogues and greetings in the market-places' (v. 43). But we dare not stand in judgment. The same trap that they fell into awaits any Christian leader who allows pride to bring about a fall.

The Problem of Insecurity

In their insecurity people look for props and props soon become idols. An insecure congregation or group can allow their minister to become a prop and, in the course of time, an idol. The expectations placed upon a minister can be considerable. Not infrequently, the same expectations can create an unhealthy dependence by the local church on its leader. Both congregation and minister develop a false sense of security. It is not difficult for a preacher to fall into the temptation of feeding his own need of acceptance and esteem by what and by how he preaches. He will know how to say certain things in a certain way which will guarantee an approving, reverential response. By doing this, though, he is only telling the congregation what they want to hear. As a result they are never confronted with the whole counsel of the word of God which comes to challenge and judge, as well as to comfort and encourage.

A group or committee in a church can become unhealthily dependent upon its leaders and the leaders upon them. Both cling to each other in a way that hinders spiritual growth and effectiveness. Most churches have groups that have long outlived their usefulness, or which need to look away from themselves and be far more concerned for others.

Christian leaders can run into the danger of allowing others to be over-dependent upon them. This can be particularly apparent in a counselling. 'You are the only one who can answer my problems' should be a warning light, but instead it can bolster pride. Serious difficulties then arise. Idol worship is at its most subtle and most dangerous in the whole area of personal relationships.

How can the peril of pride and the problem of insecurity be countered in order to prevent the deifying of Christian leaders?

The Antidote of Humility

When I was first ordained I experienced a slight sense of shock
at the sudden transition from being a theological student to
becoming a minister. Wearing a collar the wrong way round
seemed to incite some people to believe that I had all the
answers! I don't think this quite convinced me that I was God's
answer to the needs of the Church, but it was a strong warning
to walk humbly with God. Like others, I have come a cropper
when I have forgotten that. The longer I have been involved
in Christian leadership, the more I realise how little I do know
and how much I am dependent on a God who abhors pride
but gives wisdom to the humble.

The difficulty with humility is that you can be proud of being
humble! This can lead to the kind of fawning subservience that
made Uriah Heep so obnoxious. The humility that is the anti-
dote to pride is that seen in the life of the young David, who
was anointed by Samuel to succeed Saul as king. A 'nobody'
in the eyes of his family, David was a 'somebody' in the eyes
of God. Out in the Judaean hills the youthful shepherd had
developed a relationship with the Lord which knitted their
hearts as one. David possessed a humility and a readiness to
obey that enabled God to use him mightily as a future King
of Israel. David had a malleable heart — a heart that was adapt-
able and pliable to God and the direction of his Spirit.

Six days after the announcement that he was to be the next
Archbishop of Westminster, the Abbot of Ampleforth, Basil
Hume, said in a sermon to his fellow Benedictine monks:

The gap between what is thought and expected of me, and
what I know myself to be, is considerable and frightening.
There are moments in life when a man feels very small, and
in all my life this is one such moment. It is good to feel
small, for I know that whatever I achieve will be God's
achievement, not mine.[32]

Christian leadership, at whatever level, is only effective when human weakness is acknowledged and divine power relied upon.

When they reached the town of Lystra on their first missionary journey, Paul and Barnabas were the centre of adulation following the healing of a man who was lame from birth. 'The gods have come down to us in human form!' everyone shouted. (Acts 14:11). They called Barnabas Zeus and Paul Hermes and wanted to offer sacrifices to them. But Barnabas and Paul would have none of this idolatry. Their paramount concern was to point away from themselves to God. 'Men, why are you doing this? We too are only men, human like you. We are bringing you good news, telling you to turn from these worthless things to the living God' (v. 15).

Dr. Billy Graham describes his deep feeling of inadequacy for the task that lay ahead when he was on the boat coming across to England in 1954 for the London Crusade at Harringay.

> Almost night and day I prayed. I knew in a new way what Paul was telling us when he spoke about 'praying without ceasing'. Then one day in a prayer meeting with my wife and colleagues, a break came. As I wept before the Lord, I was filled with deep assurance that power belonged to God and He was faithful. From that moment on I was confident that God the Holy Spirit was in control.[33]

I was one of many thousands on the receiving end during that Crusade. I had a few days leave from the army and went with a friend, mainly out of curiosity, to hear Billy Graham speak. Though I owe much to praying parents and to the influence of school chapel services, in no way did my faith in God radically affect my life. My search for a leader who could give meaning and purpose in life was met that evening when I committed my life to Christ. When later I was to meet the girl who was to become my wife, it was to discover that she too had become a Christian at Harringay. We both thank God for the faithful ministry of Billy Graham over the years and for the humility which is a characteristic of all truly great men and women of God.

Those who walk humbly with God also walk humbly with others. This is the humility that is able to accept the honest comment and criticism of others. It is the willingness to seek the advice and check of those who know us best and who are not afraid to speak their minds with discerning love. The leader who is always on the defensive is far more likely to grow into a petty dictator than to gain the confidence and respect of others. The Book of Ecclesiastes reminds us, 'It is better to heed a wise man's rebuke than to listen to the song of fools' (7:5).

The Medicine of Laughter

There is always a strong temptation for Christian leaders to take themselves far too seriously. An inflated sense of self-importance is a snare to avoid. The pompous or deadly serious leader casts a gloom on himself as well as on others. Learning to laugh at ourselves helps to restore a better balance to life and when you are laughing it is difficult to balance on a pedestal!

The clergy of the Diocese of St. Albans owe a debt of gratitude to a far-sighted benefactor who made provision for every minister to receive, on a rota basis, a copy of the weekly magazine *Punch*. When it came to our turn, my wife and I used to read it at the end of the day and it was not long before everything else fell back into perspective! There is a wholesome power in the medicine of laughter.

> Praise to God in the highest!
> Bless us, O Father! Praise to you!
> Guide and prosper the nations,
> rulers and peoples. Praise you!
> May the truth in its beauty flourish
> triumphant.
> May the mills bring us bread
> for food and for giving.
> May the good be availed and

evil be conquered.
Give us laughter and set all
your people rejoicing.
Peace on earth and goodwill
be ever among us.

(Old Russian Prayer)

The Perspective of Pilgrimage

When people, places or objects are allowed to become idols, the sense of momentum in our Christian pilgrimage is lost. Idols either tie us to the past or shackle us in the present. If a Christian leader has become proud and self-sufficient and has developed an attitude of unapproachable infallibility, then he will have lost touch with God. Not for nothing were the disciples first called 'followers of the Way'. They knew they hadn't arrived. But they were pilgrims who, like the Israelites of old, had to be ready to strike tent and move on to the next stage of their journey. The Christian leader best guards against idolatry in himself and in others whom he leads by always being ready to follow where God leads.

On Sunday, December 13th, 1981, hurricane winds, measured at 120–150 m.p.h., swept through our Lee Abbey estate and within only a few hours, acres of trees were brought crashing down or broken like matchsticks. Many of the trees were over a hundred years old and when the winds had dropped the estate looked like a battlefield. The effect on the Community was numbing and bewildering. We had felt a justifiable pride in an estate, largely forest, which has given such joy to thousands of visitors over the years. There is always a danger in reading too much into a 'natural disaster' but we did begin to see that one lesson that God might be wanting to teach us was to beware of idolatry. Even an estate of great beauty could become an idol, something we sought to preserve for less than the highest motives. We were reminded again that power belongs to God and that the created must always point to the Creator. Furthermore, we were reminded that God is always wanting to do something new and we began to look for and see the signs of new life and new possibility where the hurricane had struck.

God will always challenge any form of idolatry. If we allow props and idols to obscure our vision of him and his glory, he leaves us behind. We may believe that we are indispensable but God is under no such illusion. He buries his workmen but carries on his work.

Chapter 15

FACING THE COST

'If you can't take it, you shouldn't have joined!', the parish clerk would sometimes retort. Invariably it made us both explode with laughter and life would be back into perspective again. But getting life into perspective for anyone who is in a position of leadership must mean that a cost has to be accepted. Are we willing to face the cost of leadership?

Loneliness

There is an inevitable loneliness in leadership. However much a leader is supported by loved ones and delegates to others, the final responsibility falls on his or her shoulders. A pre-requisite for anyone aspiring to leadership is a pair of broad shoulders!

Jesus knew the loneliness of leadership. He who had chosen twelve men to be with him, and to train for future leadership, had to experience the loneliness of being out in front, the shepherd leading his sheep. In the Garden of Gethsemane his mounting sense of loneliness is fully exposed. After his agonizing prayer of surrender to the will of his Father, he returned to the disciples and found them asleep. 'Could you men not keep watch with me for one hour?' (Matt. 26:40). It was not long afterwards that 'everyone deserted him and fled' (Mark 14:50), and there was no escaping the appalling loneliness of crucifixion on a Roman gibbet for all the world to see.

Paul's Gethsemane came when he was on trial for his life in Rome. His agony was different from Christ's, yet like his master he had to face his ordeal alone. At the time of his greatest need he wrote to Timothy from his prison cell: 'No-one came to my support, but everyone deserted me.' (2 Tim. 4:16). His one human consolation was the beloved physician: 'Only Luke is with me' (v. 11). Nevertheless, both Jesus and Paul knew that, though human support might fail, God was with them. Jesus had said to his disciples, 'You will leave me all alone. Yet I am not alone, for my Father is with me' (John 16:32). Similarly, Paul was able to say in one breath, 'Everyone deserted me' and in the next breath, 'but the Lord stood at my side and gave me strength' (2 Tim. 4:16–17).

Loneliness comes to the leader in many different forms. A decision may have to be taken which only the leader can finally make. A policy or principle may have to be defended which may incur misunderstanding or even opposition. A church or group member may have to be confronted because he has caused hurt or damage to others. A sudden emergency or tragedy may have to be squarely faced.

When I was a young curate I ran a hockey team in our youth club. Expertise varied but team-spirit was high and we enjoyed ourselves enormously. On one occasion, we were returning in a number of cars from an away match and one of the cars crashed. Michael died a short while afterwards. I shall never forget the deep sorrow and great courage of his Christian parents. Nor shall I forget my own numbing sense of loneliness. Since then, there have been many other occasions when I have had to face and accept that to lead can be a lonely role, but none has made the same mark upon me as the death of Michael.

One important qualification needs to be made. Loneliness in leadership can be self-inflicted. There are some clergy and other Christian leaders who prefer to be loners and deny themselves the support that is ready to be offered. We have seen already that 'one man band' leadership has no backing from the New Testament nor will it do anything else than stifle the spiritual life and potential growth of a local church.

Criticism

Christian leaders will always be in the firing-line of criticism. It is unavoidable. Human nature looks for someone to blame and those in positions of responsibility are prime targets. None of us would instinctively choose to be criticised but God uses both negative and constructive criticism as means whereby he gives added strength to our characters and improves the quality of our leadership.

Jesus had continually to absorb negative criticism from the Pharisees and Sadducees. Nothing he did was right in their eyes. They watched his every move and used the knife of criticism at the slightest excuse. Luke tells us that on one occasion, 'The Pharisees and the teachers of the law were looking for a reason to accuse Jesus, so they watched him closely to see if he would heal on the Sabbath' (Luke 6:7). Undeterred, Jesus healed a man who had a shrivelled right hand, much to the chagrin of his critics who began to plot how they might get rid of him. Notice how cleverly Jesus exposed the inconsistency at the heart of their criticism ... 'I ask you, which is lawful on the Sabbath: to do good or to do evil, to save life or to destroy it?' (v. 9).

Concentrated negative criticism can be very painful and potentially destructive. Where possible, it needs to be confronted and dealt with as courteously and as firmly as possible. The process of doing this can be physically, emotionally and spiritually exhausting. A Christian leader on the receiving end of intensive negative criticism should seek the prayer support, wisdom and encouragement of mature Christians who are fully aware of the facts from within the situation and of others outside it who can offer objective counsel.

Positive criticism, hard enough though it can be to accept, is a different matter. The initial reaction is to defend ourselves and even to hit back. But on further reflection, positive criticism can be welcomed as a constructive means of personal spiritual growth. In the first place, the criticism needs to be brought into our prayers so that we are able to view it in the light of

God's presence where pride and self-justification have to yield and be broken.

Secondly, the critic has to be faced. 'None of you should think only of his own affairs but should learn to see things from other people's point of view' (Phil. 2:4, J. B. Phillips). We can only see things from other people's point of view if we are prepared to discuss the reasons for their criticism with them and not be slow or afraid to acknowledge where there is justification. Accepting criticism of our faults and blind spots often needs to be followed by asking forgiveness. In this way relationships are strengthened and not severed. Confidence in our leadership may even be increased rather than lessened.

On one occasion I was present when a leader was receiving criticism from a group member. I much admired the way the points of conflict were raised, discussed and faced. It revealed both the courage of the critic and the humility of the leader who was able to accept the criticism. In the process the critic realised that he too had to put things right.

Jack Boggs, Pastor of Suffolk Baptist Church, Fedge Fen, said, 'Our assignment is to please God, to live critically before him, rather than to please others by living un-criticised by them. If criticism stops we are dead. Criticism is strong affirmation. It proves we are alive. Take courage, wounded warrior, no-one criticised the obituary column!'

Suffering

For the follower of Christ the reality of suffering cannot be avoided. The sign of Christian discipleship is not a crib or a crown but a cross. We rejoice that 'the tree of shame has become the tree of glory' but this must not blind us to all that the Cross of Christ has to say about suffering. The Christian leader dare not leave out the element of suffering when teaching others what could be involved in being a Christian.

When a Baptism takes place in an Anglican Church, the minister declares, 'I sign you with the Cross, the sign of Christ.

Do not be ashamed to confess the faith of Christ crucified.' Everyone present then replies, 'Fight valiantly under the banner of Christ against sin, the world and the devil, and continue his faithful soldier and servant to the end of your life.' From the start to the finish of Christian pilgrimage suffering is implicit for those who are prepared to go the way of the Cross.

There are, of course, many different causes and forms of suffering. There is the suffering that comes as a result of our own sinfulness and wilfulness, or the sin and selfishness of others. Then there is the suffering that is the experience of our common humanity, such as sickness or bereavement. For the Christian there is also the suffering which comes as a result of standing up for what we believe, whether in opposing evil and injustice or because we have different values and standards. In Britain and the West physical suffering as a Christian is rare, but to be unashamed to confess the faith of Christ crucified may bring ridicule, ostracism and even the loss of a job.

If suffering is part of the cost of our calling as Christians, how are we to face it?

First, we need to accept suffering as something allowed and entrusted to us. To the Philippian Christians Paul wrote, 'For it has been granted to you on behalf of Christ not only to believe on him, but also to suffer for him' (1:29). Much pain and bitterness is caused through the non-acceptance of suffering. Often the question 'Why?' goes unanswered, but the way forward is to trust that the God who is our Father and who has allowed it to happen is in ultimate control. Many Christians have proved the truth of Cardinal Mercier's words: 'Suffering accepted and vanquished will give you a serenity which may well prove the most exquisite fruit of your life.'

Second, suffering needs to be shared. In stark contrast to his impeccable pedigree as a high-born Jew, Paul declares that now he has only one ambition. 'I want to know Christ and the power of his resurrection and the fellowship of sharing in his sufferings, becoming like him in his death, and so, somehow, to attain to the resurrection from the death' (Phil. 3: v. 10–11).

We share the sufferings of Christ wherever his Body, the Church, is suffering. The persecuted South Korean, Cardinal Kin, wrote,

> There are many kinds of bread. There is the good, white bread of friendship, but there is also the black bread of suffering, of loneliness, and of poverty. This is the bread in which splinters of wood have been mixed. This black bread of suffering should be fraternally divided.

In our own churches and fellowships we are to share one another's sufferings. No one should be allowed to suffer alone; 'if one member suffers, all suffer together'.

Third, there is glory and victory through suffering. In the New Testament, suffering and glory are often linked together. 'Now if we are children, then we are heirs – heirs of God and co-heirs with Christ, if indeed we share in his sufferings in order that we may also share in his glory' (Rom. 8:17).

Martinhoe is a small village on the North Devon coast. The thirteenth century church of St. Martin contains a plaque erected by its rector and his wife in the last century:

> To the beloved memory of
> three sons of the Rev. Charles Scrivers,
>   Rector of this parish,
> and Fanny Sarah, his wife.
>
> Charles Edward, eldest son
>   Died Aug. 21 1877. Aged 28 years
>
> William B.A. Oxford, second son
>   Died May 8 1877. Aged 27 years
>
> George Canning, fourth son
>   Died at Cape Town, Jan 1 1878.
>   Aged 23 years
>
> 'They shall be mine, saith the Lord, in that day when I make up my jewels.'

This simple plaque conveys both the poignant suffering of this Christian family and their sure hope of future glory.

Discouragement

Discouragement has claimed many casualties among the ranks of those who have had some share in leadership in the local church. The temptation to give up is difficult to resist when the Sunday School teacher has a dwindling number of children on the roll, or when the youth club leader is trying to cope with an unresponsive and unruly group of young people intent on wrecking the premises. Nor is it easy for the minister always to swallow discouragement when he works his heart out with little or no result. There are many churches in rural and inner-city areas whose leaders and tiny congregations are bowed down by discouragement and disappointment and wonder how long they can survive.

Every Christian leader, however successful, feels the full force of the chilling wind of discouragement. Those we lead will sometimes disappoint us by not fulfilling our hopes. For one reason or another some hold back from whole-hearted Christian commitment or drift away altogether. In turn, it is not difficult to be discouraged by our own failure to come up to our own expectation, let alone God's. Yet the acceptance of discouragement as an inevitable part of the cost of leadership is essential. What matters is that we don't wallow in it but learn to overcome discouragement.

Caleb has been aptly described as the Mr. Greatheart of the Old Testament. His outstanding characteristic was his refusal to be diminished by discouragement. Instead, he kept his eyes fixed on God and his purpose for the people of Israel. He first came into prominence when, as a leader of the tribe of Judah, he was chosen to be one of the twelve spies sent out to explore the Promised Land of Canaan.

At the end of forty days the spies returned and two conflicting reports were presented to Moses and the people. The majority report by ten of the spies warned that the cities were too well defended and the Canaanites too powerful for an invasion to be successful. The minority report by Caleb and Joshua urged the Israelites to go forward. 'We should go up and take possession of the land, for we can certainly do it' (Num. 13:30). The majority report won the day and forty years of aimless wandering in the wilderness followed. A lesson, perhaps, to take minority reports seriously!

Caleb, however, was unbowed by discouragement and frustration. When eventually the Israelites were poised to enter Canaan, Caleb was there by the side of the new leader, his friend Joshua. When most men would have put on their carpet slippers, Caleb was as vigorous and purposeful as ever. His faith in the living God had remained unwavering. No obstacles were too great. He had implicit confidence in the power and greatness of his God with whom nothing was impossible. It is little wonder that God's estimate of Caleb was 'My servant Caleb . . . follows me wholeheartedly' (Num. 14:24).

The story of Caleb is a reminder that older Christian leaders can be an enormous encouragement to younger leaders during periods of discouragement. By their accumulated experience of God's faithfulness through thick and thin, they can help the younger leader to see their own times of discouragement and testing in true perspective. Those who have proved God's faithfulness during the course of a long life have a vital role to play in the life of the local church. Younger people are encouraged by the example, and benefit from the wisdom, of older Christians whose faith has stood the test of time and changing circumstances and who remain eager to discover more and more about God. William Barclay tells of receiving a letter which concluded with: 'Yours, eighty-three years old and still growing.'

My wife and I will not forget the encouragement that Percy Stevens, who had been a bishop in China, used to bring whenever he stayed with us in the early 1960s. He was then over eighty but his physical energy, mental agility and spiritual vitality were a tonic and a challenge. He would get up early in the morning for a time alone with God and we would often hear him singing psalms! He was a Caleb to us and we thank God for his infectious faith.

The leader who remains true to Jesus will have the Cross fixed in his heart. Accepting the cost of leadership is accepting identification with Christ in his passion and death.

A leader needs to bear the print of the nails — the marks of sacrifice. Except others see the print of the nails they will not believe. Until they see the authentic marks of Christ in us whom they can see, they will never believe in a Christ whom they cannot see. Let none that aspire to lead in the name of Christ slide subtly into the treason that thinks to soften the rough realities of the Cross. The Cross is the sign of the utmost love — of a love that gives all, that withholds nothing. This is the price of leadership.[34]

(A. E. Norrish)

Those who are prepared to face the cost of leadership discover the truth of Jesus's words, 'If any man would come after me, let him deny himself and take up his cross and follow me. For whoever would save his life will lose it, and whoever loses his life for my sake will find it.' (Matt. 16:24,25).

Chapter 16

FINAL ACCOUNTABILITY

'The buck stops here' stated the notice on the desk of a former President of the United States of America. Few people find it difficult to enjoy the privileges and the power that often come with leadership. Many shrink from, or try to minimise, its responsibilities. Yet the acceptance of the responsibilities of leadership, whether they be small or large, is a necessary part of recognising the importance of accountability. The Christian leader needs to remember that he or she is accountable – to God and to others.

At the close of a retreat that I had been conducting for clergy from the diocese of Pretoria, the Bishop knelt silently in the centre, acknowledging his accountability both to God and to those who looked to him for leadership. He asked that we should all pray for him and black, coloured and white hands were laid on him in loving response. It was a sacred moment. We were joined together in a common bond. This same bond of accountability, availability in his service and dependence on his resources, unites all who respond to God's call to leadership.

Will You?

The acceptance of accountability doesn't come easily. It demands a dogged stickability when the going is tough and pressures are mounting. It rebukes self-pity and the temptation to be softer with ourselves and harder with others. It seeks to stiffen self-control when an inner desire for assertion is threatening to break out in resentment and even rebellion against those to whom we are answerable. It acts as a steady, persistent reminder that those who lead others dare not do so irresponsibly.

On the one hand, accountability provides a necessary and healthy safeguard against the strident misuse or abuse of position and power. On the other hand, it serves to challenge the half-heartedness of timidity that wants to opt out of fulfilling responsibilities. Moreover, it offers a framework of sanction in which the leader can operate with a sense of confidence and freedom. As in many other areas of life freedom comes, not by throwing off restraints, but by accepting their legitimacy and welcoming the supportive strengths they give to those who lead.

Ultimately, a Christian leader is accountable to God. Jesus stressed this in a number of parables. In the Parable of the Talents (Matt. 25:14–30), the servants who were entrusted with their Master's property were given varying responsibilities. Two of them, who were given five and two talents respectively, were not slow to accept their accountability. They doubled their money and their wise stewardship gained their Master's commendation on his return. 'Well done, good and faithful servant! You have been faithful with a few things; I will put you in charge of many things. Come and share your master's happiness!' (v. 23). In contrast, the servant who had been given one talent, dug a hole in the ground and hid his master's money. His indolence and lame excuses received the condemnation they deserved. He had ignored his accountability.

Accountability is an incentive to live each day, to care for each person, and do each job to the best of our ability; not striving for a perfection that drives us and others into the ground, but ensuring that we offer our best to God. James Galway, the Irishman with the dancing eyes and the magic flute, describes the attitudes that crystallised for him after a serious accident when he broke his legs and sustained other injuries:

I decided that henceforward I would play every concert, cut every record, give every television performance, as though it were my last. I've come to understand that it is never possible to guess what might happen next; that the roof might fall in any time and that the important thing is to make sure that every time I play the flute my performance will be as near perfection and full of true music as God intended, and that I shall not be remembered for a shoddy performance. My ambitions, therefore, are limited. They are merely that I should leave good memories behind me; that people should feel when they recall my name, that in some odd, inexplicable way, they have at some time heard the voice of the infinite through me.[35]

God never gives us responsibilities that are beyond our capabilities. Rather, he expects us to use and develop our talents to the full. For those in the early stages of leadership this will mean learning how to be accountable for smaller tasks and resources. 'Do what you can, and the task will rest lightly in your hands. So lightly that you will be able to look forward to the more difficult tasks that may be awaiting you' (Dag Hammarskjöld).[36] Unless we are faithful in the lesser things God entrusts to us, he will not entrust us with anything greater. One of the temptations in leadership is to want to tackle more responsibility without first completing the assigned job as competently and conscientiously as possible. The grass always seems greener on the other side of the fence!

Many a prominent Christian leader today laid strong foundations in the past by setting high priority on the way smaller responsibilities were tackled in comparative obscurity. Former members of the Lee Abbey Community, now in positions of leadership in different parts of the world, learnt that cleaning a toilet, scrubbing a kitchen floor, handling a booking enquiry, or harvesting silage provided invaluable lessons in doing every task, however unglamorous, to the best of their ability and to the glory of God. 'Whatever you do, whether in word or deed, do it all in the name of the Lord Jesus, giving thanks to God the Father through him' (Col. 3:17).

Did You?

There comes the time when every Christian leader has to render an account to God for what has been done in the name of Christ. I find this both an awesome and a welcome thought. Awesome, because like other leaders I know only too well my huge areas of failure and disobedience. Welcome, because the knowledge that I am answerable to God for everyone and everything entrusted to me helps to keep me on my toes. Leaders are stewards. We can call nothing our own. Everything we are and everything we have is a gift of God, who rightly expects a full account of our stewardship.

In a preordination charge, Dr. Donald Coggan began with these words:

> Your preordination training is over. Your retreat is nearly over. Tomorrow you will be ordained. You come to that great service in hope — and trembling. To you, tomorrow, will come the solemn words: 'Take thou authority . . .' To you will be addressed the questions, 'Will you?' 'Will you?' One day God will ask, 'Did you?' 'Did you?'[37]

The certainty of that day of final accountability puts any sphere of leadership into proper perspective. It reminds us that 'My Sunday School class' or 'My choir' or 'My youth club' or 'My home group' or 'My congregation' are a trust from God. In fact, as we have seen in earlier chapters, the New Testament pattern of leadership seeks to emphasise corporate as well as personal responsibility. Whether it be 'our' or 'my' it is God to whom we are ultimately responsible. He it is who calls men and women into leadership. To respond to that call is to take our part in sharing the love of God with those we lead and helping prepare them for heaven. What a privilege! What a responsibility!

God with Us

Travelling through the Sinai desert recently I couldn't help marvelling at the way Moses sustained such a high degree of responsibility for the Israelites. In the face of constant set-backs, flagrant disobedience and sheer ingratitude, he somehow never lost sight of his accountability to the God who had placed the onus of leadership upon his shoulders.

At one point Moses was overwhelmed by the magnitude of his task. He had returned from Mount Sinai with the ten commandments to find that the people of Israel were besotted with the worship of a golden calf, and were running wild. His anger and disappointment boiled over. It all seemed so pointless. He felt acutely the deep sense of failure and frustration that every leader experiences at one time or another. 'How can I possibly go on leading this stubborn, rebellious people?', he must have asked himself again and again.

Wisely, Moses didn't bottle it all up within himself but talked it over with God in the Tent of Meeting:

Moses said to the Lord, 'You have been telling me, "lead these people", but you have not let me know whom you will send with me. You have said, "I know you by name and you have found favour with me." If I have found favour in your eyes, teach me your ways so I may know you and continue to find favour with you. Remember that this nation is your people.' The Lord replied, 'My Presence will go with you, and I will give you rest.'

(Exodus 33:12–14)

The assurance that God was with him reinforced Moses' strength and courage and with fresh determination he pressed on.

The Church is in urgent need of more leaders. In many local churches the position is critical. Vacancies for key positions of responsibility are waiting to be filled. I cannot believe that the stock of potential leaders has come to an end. Rather, I suggest that the national disease of avoiding responsibility has affected the attitude of many Christians who should be coming forward. One thing is certain. The opportunities confronting the local church are enormous but, if they are to be seized, leaders must be found, trained and fully used. Leaders are wanted whose lives convincingly reflect the love of Jesus and who see their role as servants, encouragers and enablers.

To those who are prepared to accept the call and challenge of leadership God's promise remains the same: 'My Presence will go with you.' It is a promise that holds fast through the inevitable 'downs' and 'ups', through adversity and adventure. When God is with us all things become possible. He never forgets his responsibility towards us.

'The One who calls you is faithful and he will do it' (1 Thess. 5:24).

REFERENCES

1   *The Shoes of the Fisherman*, Morris West (Fontana)
2   *Letters from the Desert*, Carlo Carretto (DLT)
3   *The Good Shepherd*, Lesslie Newbigin (Faith Press)
4   *The Reformed Pastor*, Richard Baxter
5   *Testament of Faith*, William Barclay (Mowbrays)
6   Hymn, 'Rock of Ages', Augustus M. Toplady, 1740–78
7   *A Gift of God*, Mother Teresa (Collins)
8   *Life Together*, Dietrich Bonhoeffer (SCM Press)
9   Prayer of St. Augustine
10 *Silence*, Religious Society of Friends (Quakers)
11 *Rule of Taize*, Brother Roger Schulz (Les Presses de Taize)
12 Hymn, 'O Worship the Lord', John S. B. Monsell, 1811–75
13 *Testament of Faith*, William Barclay (Mowbrays)
14 *Holiness*, J. C. Ryle (James Clarke and Co)
15 *I Believe in Church Growth*, Eddie Gibbs (Hodder and Stoughton)
16 *Community and Growth*, Jean Vanier (DLT)
17 *My Life*, Golda Meir, Weidenfeld and Nicolson
18 *The Go-Between God*, John V. Taylor (SCM Press)
19 *A Question of Conscience*, Charles Davis (Hodder and Stoughton)
20 *Cost of Discipleship*, Dietrich Bonhoeffer (SCM Press)
21 *Letters to Young Churches*, J. B. Phillips (Geoffrey Bless Ltd
22 *Taste of New Wine*, Keith Miller (Word Publications)
23 'The Servant Song', Richard Gillard (Copyright Permission May '82, Marshall, Morgan and Scott)
24 *I Believe in the Great Commission*, Max Warren (Hodder and Stoughton)
25 *Dick Sheppard*, Carolyn Scott (Hodder and Stoughton)

26 *The Adventure of Living*, Paul Tournier (SCM Press)
27 *The Memoirs of Field-Marshal Montgomery* (Fontana)
28 *Nothing Venture, Nothing Win*, Edmund Hillary (Hodder and Stoughton)
29 *I Believe in the Church*, David Watson (Hodder and Stoughton)
30 *The Call to Conversion*, Jim Wallis (Lion Publishers)
31 Hymn, 'O For a Closer Walk with God', William Cowper, 1731–1800
32 *Searching for God*, Basil Hume (Hodder and Stoughton)
33 *The Holy Spirit*, Billy Graham (Fount)
34 *Christian Leadership*, A. E. Norrish, (New Delhi Publishers)
35 *An Autobiography*, James Galway (Coronet/Hodder and Stoughton)
36 *Markings*, Dag Hammarskjöld (Faber and Faber)
37 *Convictions*, Donald Coggan (Hodder and Stoughton)